D0463583

Real Estate Riches

A Canadian Investor's Guide to Working with the Right Agent

Tahani Aburaneh

WILEY

John Wiley & Sons Canada, Ltd.

Library and Archives Canada Cataloguing in Publication

Aburaneh, Tahani, 1965–

Real estate riches : a Canadian investor's guide to working with the right agent / Tahani Aburaneh.

Includes index.

Issued also in electronic formats.

ISBN 978-0-470-96421-7

1. Real estate investment. 2. Real estate agents. I. Title.

HD1382.5.A28 2012   332.63'24   C2011-905605-4

ISBN 978-0-470-93771-6 (ePub); 978-0-470-93773-0 (eMobi); 978-0-470-93770-9 (ePDF)

Production Credits
Cover design: Pat Loi
Interior design: Thomson Digital
Typesetter: Thomson Digital
Printer: Friesens

Editorial Credits
Executive Editor: Don Loney
Production Editor: Jeremy Hanson-Finger

John Wiley & Sons Canada, Ltd.
6045 Freemont Blvd.
Mississauga, Ontario
L5R 4J3

Printed in Canada

1 2 3 4 5 FP 16 15 14 13 12

ENVIRONMENTAL BENEFITS STATEMENT

John Wiley & Sons - Canada saved the following resources by printing the pages of this book on chlorine free paper made with 100% post-consumer waste.

TREES	WATER	ENERGY	SOLID WASTE	GREENHOUSE GASES
45	20,637	18	1,308	4,577
FULLY GROWN	GALLONS	MILLION BTUs	POUNDS	POUNDS

Environmental impact estimates were made using the Environmental Paper Network Paper Calculator. For more information visit www.papercalculator.org.

Table of Contents

Acknowledgments

I am deeply grateful to so many who have helped make this book possible. I feel so blessed to be able to share my knowledge with thousands of Canadians.

Special thanks to Don R. Campbell, president of the Real Estate Investment Network, for believing in me and what I could offer the world of real estate investing. It is truly because of you that this book came to life.

And to Don Loney, executive editor at John Wiley & Sons Canada, Ltd. and his team. Writing a book is not an easy undertaking, but Don was there every step of the way. His insight, creative suggestions, positive attitude, and support made this experience a most pleasurable one. Thank you, Don.

To Wayne Karl, thank you for your talent in putting together all these words, for crafting the manuscript, for keeping me on track, and for all your support each and every day. What a journey this has been.

My daughter, Suraya, and son, Ramsey, I am so fortunate to have such amazing, encouraging, and supportive kids in my life.

To my sister, Hanady, with your wisdom, insight, and love, I am able to be here in my life. I love you so much.

And a special thank-you to all the contributors to this book who have put in the time, effort and expertise to give back and help out. Just like the real estate business, writing a book is all about teamwork. I thank you all.

Foreword

CAN WE ALL JUST GET ALONG?

I have been analyzing and investing in the Canadian real estate market for over 20 years and have often shaken my head at the disconnect between two parties that have the same goals and objectives—yet don't seem to see eye to eye. Those two groups are sophisticated real estate investors and realtors. Both want to move or buy quality properties, both want to make money doing so, and both want not to waste precious time in doing so.

In most other professions, business owners look for long-term clientele who consistently buy the company's product. Yet in real estate, in more cases than not, realtors are disinclined to work with professional real estate investors, despite the fact that investors consistently want to buy properties and eventually sell them. (Yes, I know, this perception of investors doesn't make any sense to me either.)

That being said, the professional real estate agents who discover the income-generating secret of adding a few professional real estate investors to their client list are often at, or near, the top of their real estate board's income and volume leaders.

Sure, there are many "seminar grads" who purport to be professional real estate investors. These are the people who waste a professional agent's time by not being clear in what they are looking for, and they haven't even narrowed down their target areas. These so-called investors haven't done their homework and expect the agent to do it all for them. These are the people who ruin the reputation of all investors with realtors.

What this all means is that both investors and agents have a tremendous opportunity for financial success if they shift how they work with each other, respect each other's profession, and do whatever it takes to make the other party successful. In my many years of investing, I (and fellow sophisticated investors of the Real Estate Investment Network™) have made a select few realtors very successful. We are clear with our realtors, we complete our own due diligence and, most importantly, we close on properties when a realtor brings us one that fits our model. These realtors have come to understand the efficiencies in creating residual income by working on and building a solid relationship with a select few investors who will buy a number of properties per year versus home buyers who may buy one every five years

This book really shows both professional investors and professional agents how, if done right, both parties can come out with better financial results with less hassle by treating the real estate business like any other business—creating long-term relationships in which each party respects the other's profession and treats each other's time like the important commodity that it is.

Here's to building business!

Don R. Campbell
Bestselling Author, Market Analyst & Investor
www.DonRCampbell.com

Introduction

Why wait to invest in real estate? Instead, invest in real estate and wait.

How about this for a modern-day fairy tale? Born into humble beginnings in a far-off land, an independent mother of two becomes a self-made millionaire in her new home—Canada—within a few short years. Well, it's true. And my passion for helping others realize their potential, guiding them to overcome financial obstacles, and nurturing their dreams and aspirations led to this book.

Welcome to *Real Estate Riches*.

WHAT THIS BOOK WILL DO FOR YOU

By acting on the ideas and strategies in this book, you will take the initial step to improving your financial future by investing in real estate (if you're a first-timer) or to expanding your portfolio (if you're already an investor). This book is about helping you, step by step, develop the mindset and know-how to make wise investments in rental properties. We will look at your motives for investing in real estate and any underlying assumptions you may have about real estate, how an investor-savvy agent can be a valuable asset, how to buy your first investment property, and how to buy additional properties.

Real Estate Riches will have you moving comfortably and confidently toward becoming a sophisticated real estate investor. I aim to help not just by sharing my story and knowledge but also by sharing the wisdom of many of my colleagues who also understand the importance of real estate investing.

You may be a first-time investor looking for a guide; perhaps you currently own a primary residence plus one or two investment properties, and have decided to grow your real estate business by expanding your holdings; or maybe you are looking for systems that will help you become a more knowledgeable investor. If you've done well so far—by luck, circumstance, or instinct—you may want to protect and grow your assets and net worth by acquiring additional properties in a more sophisticated manner, but aren't quite sure how to go about doing that.

Real Estate Riches will help you with all of that. I promise you that by the time you've finished reading this book, you will have the knowledge and information you need to get started as a sophisticated real estate investor. And if you still have questions, I invite you to contact me directly through my website, www.realestateHchesbook.com.

MY STORY

By now you may be wondering who I am. Who is Tahani Aburaneh, and how can she help me?

In many ways, I am just like you, only a few years further along in the real estate business, thanks to lots of ambition, hard work, and a few well-timed deals.

Let me tell you about my humble beginnings, not because I am bold, but because it's important to show you where I've come from to get here and to give you the inspiration, drive, and confidence to become a successful investor, no matter what your starting point.

If you *believe*, you will *achieve*.

In the interest of full disclosure, at this point I should clarify that I am not only a real estate *investor*, I am also a *realtor*—and one who specializes in working with investors. I am very passionate about working with both first-time and experienced investors, because I have seen the difference successfully investing in real estate makes to their confidence and to their pocketbooks.

In working with investors, I have seen it all—from the "action takers" to those who read tons of books and attend courses, but can't get out there and take action and *buy*, because they feel they still need to learn more before taking that first step.

The best way to learn, I have found, is by *doing*.

I operate my own brokerage, Key Connexions (www.keyconnexions.ca), in my adopted hometown of Cambridge, Ontario, which, coincidentally, is one of the top real estate investment regions in the province and, in fact, all of Canada. I started out as a realtor selling primary homes, then became a real estate investor myself, and then an agent catering specifically to the needs of investors. And more recently, I became a developer, building my own small townhome community in Cambridge.

Young Entrepreneur

How did I get here? I was born in Amman, Jordan, into a family of very modest means, and lived in a refugee camp until my teenage years. Even as a young girl in Amman, I always had an entrepreneurial spirit, inspiring me to go "into business" for myself. I was often thinking of ways to make money. I would crochet items or bake sweets and send my brothers out to sell them. With the money I made, I would buy gold jewellery. That's how it was over there. Living in a refugee camp, there weren't homes or real estate or much else to buy, so I would buy gold. I had many gold necklaces, while other girls my age had none.

As is typical in Middle Eastern culture, I entered into an arranged marriage at a young age, and eventually immigrated to Canada in 1981, settling in the Kitchener-Waterloo area of southwestern Ontario. By the early 1990s, and in my mid-20s, I had two young children and was working with my then-husband in a variety store.

This is how my real estate career started. In 1992, my oldest brother asked me to help him open a dollar store in downtown Cambridge. I had previously opened a few small businesses, all very successful, and my entrepreneurial spirit and passion for business continued to grow.

There was a real estate office across the street from the dollar store, and the owner-broker of record would visit almost every day. He would always urge me to put my people skills and business acumen to better use in real estate—he thought I would do really well at it. I wasn't certain it was for me, so my standard answer was, "No, I can't do that." The next day, he would be back, again trying to encourage me. Finally, one day I said, "You know what? I'm going to go for it!" After all, I loved the idea of getting into business.

So, in May 1995, I joined the local Coldwell Banker office, selling resale homes. After about six months, that office closed and I moved to Century 21. Those were tough times in real estate. The market was still bouncing back from a downturn, and the industry was very different than it is now. At that time (and it wasn't really that long ago) we had to complete all offers in writing—by hand—and do a lot of driving back and forth between buyers and sellers. Few agents even had cellphones.

Calling from my office telephone wasn't too successful for me, since I had a thick accent and hadn't yet mastered my sales technique. So I hit the streets, literally knocking on doors to ask people if they were thinking of selling their homes. It took six months to sign my first listing, but I sold it quickly once I got it. It took a lot of hard work, determination, and a will to make things happen. I never once thought about giving up. If anything, it fuelled me to do well, to persist no matter what.

The Tipping Point

After a few years of selling real estate, I felt something was missing—my entrepreneurial spirit kept surfacing. The resale business was okay, but I really didn't find it that exciting.

Then came a day to remember. I was selling my brother's semi-detached house, and another realtor brought along a buyer who was looking at the property as an investment. I was intrigued by his offer, since it contained many clauses and inclusions that a typical resale offer did not. It was also confusing, since, even as a realtor, I didn't fully understand the difference in working with an investor.

The deal didn't go anywhere, but it did open my mind to the possibility of attracting and working with such investors. It unlocked something within me. Here was this client buying property as a business. I said to myself, "Real estate investing is a business?" And I thought about it more and more. It truly inspired me, and set in motion a desire to learn as much as I could about investment real estate.

Soon after, I helped a couple—the husband was a handyman—buy a house they planned to fix up and sell for a profit—what we know today as a "fix and flip." I found a property, which they bought, renovated, and flipped for a tidy profit. I was so happy to have helped them with that deal. I visited them often, and I truly felt like part of their family. This experience was so fulfilling. The challenge then became how to find similar investors and help them execute similar deals.

In 2002, my husband and I divorced, and I stepped up my game. I now had a drive to survive on my own and a need to make money so I could care for my children. Based on my experience selling resale homes for a few years, I convinced a builder in Cambridge to hire me. His wife was having limited success selling the homes on his site, so I saw it as an opportunity. "Hire me. I can make you and your wife a lot of money," I told him. In a few short months I sold 18 houses and ended up selling for three out of the four builders in that subdivision.

Interestingly, my marketing efforts for that site began attracting investors, who were asking about rental rates and vacancy rates. I didn't know much about investors, because real estate agents typically deal with homeowners. I admitted to these potential clients that I didn't have the answers to all their questions, but I was committed to finding out. I was willing to do whatever it took to get them what they needed, and they loved my go-getter personality.

My Birth as an Investor

This is what started the investor ball rolling for me: I was so intrigued by these experiences that I approached the Cambridge builder who first hired me and convinced him to sell me my first investment property, for $220,000—with only $1,000 down. (I had the good fortune of a strong relationship with this builder; I had sold a lot of homes for him, and he trusted me.)

That first purchase whetted my appetite for real estate investing. And I've never looked back. In less than six months, that $1,000 investment made me $48,000. I still own that property today, renting it out with positive cash flow, with about $100,000 in equity. That $1,000 investment has made me almost $150,000.

Over the years, I have bought and sold about 40 of my own rental homes for profit. I hold several investment properties, with plans to buy more, including multi-family units such as apartment buildings. Many of my earlier deals as an investor were flips, which, despite what some television programming would have you believe, can be quite a risky investment strategy for novice investors. I would not recommend fix and flips as a strategy for novice investors in today's economic environment.

An admission: I didn't begin understanding long-term real estate investing the way I do today until 2006, when I became a member of the Real Estate Investment Network (REIN) and started learning from Don R. Campbell.

I attended my first meeting as a guest, and I distinctly remember the experience. It was so enlightening that I signed up as a member that same night. Despite some of my earlier real estate successes, at times I felt I was under water, not completely knowledgeable of every situation. Sitting in that first REIN meeting, I felt like, "I can breathe!"

During the first few meetings, I almost felt embarrassed by how much I was learning, how little I really knew compared to the sophisticated investors in the room. How could I be a realtor when I didn't know all these things Don was teaching? I thought most of the other investors in the room were more savvy than me. It was quite a realization. I remember feeling lucky to find the network, and I feel blessed even to this day. It solidified my desire to learn and learn and learn.

Joining REIN helped me make the important step to becoming a sophisticated real estate investor—one who makes informed decisions with knowledge of local economic and real estate fundamentals, as opposed to one who goes on instinct and luck. Now, I know exactly what to look for in assessing potential areas and properties, where to find information on vacancy rates and rental rates, and more importantly, how to educate my clients and provide the best service with this expertise.

Today, I use that expertise in my career as an agent focused on real estate investors. Most of my business—about 85 per cent—is with investor-clients. Most of them typically own two to seven properties, and some many more than that. I'm even converting many of my regular home-buying clients into investors, after demonstrating the value of investing for them and their families.

Key Connexions

In 2009, I took one more important, formal step as an agent focusing on investors. I could see an opportunity—all these investors out there, but not enough realtors focused on servicing them properly—so I started my own brokerage, Key Connexions (www.keyconnexions.ca). With my background as an agent, then investor, then more sophisticated investor, and finally as an agent focused on investors, I have unique experience and skills to help investor-clients achieve their goals—because I've been through it all myself.

I recently took a further significant step—the birth of Tahani Development Inc., a company I put together to develop land and build properties.

My business also includes training realtors on how to understand and work with investors.

All of this causes me to reflect on how I've come to this point in my life and career, and how my experiences might impact other people's lives and empower them to take control of their financial situation. This is why it's important to share my story with you. I thank God every single day. I am a very, very blessed woman, and I want that blessing for you as well.

People perceive success differently. For some, the goal may be to achieve millionaire status. For others, financial stability may be enough. Whatever your ambition, my goal is to use my specialized knowledge to help you achieve success. A defiant spirit and determination have propelled me to the top of the property investment ladder. Let's get on with helping you take your first steps.

MAKING THE INVESTOR-AGENT CONNECTION

CHAPTER 1

Why You Need an Investor-Savvy Agent

If you've bought and sold a principal residence or investment property, you know how important it is to have a realtor act on your behalf during the process. He or she can help you find a property, prepare your home for sale, write offers to purchase, negotiate the purchase price, make referrals for other services, and generally guide you through the numerous steps. You could never do that with someone you didn't trust and value, right?

Now imagine that on your journey to becoming a more sophisticated investor, with more deals, properties, and dollars at stake, you're able to work with an agent who *specializes* in working with investors like yourself. Someone who, yes, can handle all the technical details of buying and selling property, but who also understands the investment side of the business— because he or she is also an investor. Someone like that can help you find an excellent buy, instead of a good one, and can help you choose a solid investment, rather than a lucky one.

How much would that be worth to you?

In any profession, be it law, medicine, or in this case, real estate, specialists provide an expertise that their more generalist colleagues do not possess. For real estate investors, investor-savvy agents are a huge asset because they intimately know all the important steps you're going to take and the information you need to make solid decisions—after all, they have acquired income-producing real estate themselves. Such experience could be the difference between an excellent and profitable buy, and one you come to regret.

THE VALUE PROPOSITION OF AN INVESTOR-SAVVY AGENT

The job of an investor-savvy realtor is to understand you, the client, as an *investor*, not just a homebuyer. Many realtors are interested in individual transactions—simply buying and selling homes and gaining commissions. Investor-savvy agents, on the other hand, understand your goals and objectives because they are investors themselves, and they have the knowledge and expertise to help you find cash-flowing properties that meet your strategy, vis-à-vis where you are in life and in your real estate investing career.

For example, I recently met with a couple that were thinking of becoming real estate investors. As soon as I began talking to them, I learned they'd bought only one house, their own home, and had been living there for 25 years. They were ready to buy investment property, and wanted to understand the different strategies they could choose from. It would have been a huge mistake for me to put them in something that didn't suit them, something fast-paced such as a fix and flip. For this couple, and for many typical first-time investors, the ideal fit would be something stable—in a stable area with stable returns—that they could buy and hold with little work. With one long-term primary residence, *stability* was the story of their lives, so a slow-moving, easy-to-manage property would be perfect for them.

For another client, a contractor who is very comfortable as a handyman, a suitable property might be one that required a little work—not necessarily to fix and flip, but a home that would benefit from a little sweat equity in painting and other cosmetic improvements, which he could provide himself, to improve cash flow and increase value.

It really depends on individual clients: their goals and strategies, financial resources, limitations, and knowledge and experience. And, of course, the essential question of why: Why do they want to invest in real estate?

"The Big Why"

Let's talk about your "why." Why do *you* want to invest in real estate? Is it to build your retirement nest egg, to pay for your kids' education, to generate extra income to pay expenses, or to replace your income entirely by becoming a full-time investor? Few people actually love bricks and mortar, but who wouldn't love financial freedom?

Whatever your "why," investor-focused agents can help you achieve your goals, because they understand investment real estate—the local market and other important factors—more than realtors who deal purely in selling primary residences. Agents selling homes only to first-time or move-up buyers simply match up potential properties to buyers' parameters for location, price, proximity to work, and other key criteria.

Searching for investment properties, on the other hand, involves a different process and another set of rules. When working with investors, realtors need to be more knowledgeable about the local market fundamentals, developments in the economy, goings-on with the municipal government, what makes one potential neighbourhood or street more desirable than another, the vacancy and rental rates for the area, and the tenant profile for the neighbourhood.

The importance of the above points cannot be overstated, and we will discuss all of them in greater detail later.

First-time or would-be investors sometimes try to make purchasing decisions based on advice from friends or relatives, what they hear or read in the media, or other information that doesn't always make for the best choices. Selecting neighbourhoods and properties to invest in requires looking for very specific trends and developments. A tip from your Uncle Fred or the friendly community butcher isn't going to (pardon the pun) cut it for you in terms of unearthing *real* investment opportunities. It may help, but it's an opinion, and quite likely not an informed opinion. When dealing with your or your family's financial future, you need expert advice.

Among the most valuable tools that licensed agents provide are reports called CMAs—comparative market analyses—also known as "comparables." This is critical information that should be closely considered when buying a property, since it details recent buying and selling activity in the neighbourhood, how long each property has been on the market, the asking and final selling prices, and other data.

Local Market Expertise

Investor-savvy agents provide critical information that you, as an investor and landlord, will want and need to know, including:

- How much could this property rent for?
- What are the average rents in this neighbourhood?
- What are the vacancy rates in this area for this type of property?
- How have rents in the area been trending over the last one to three years?
- What kind of tenant will this property attract?
- Are renters attracted to the neighbourhood?
- Is the property saleable, since one day you will likely want to sell it?
- What is the recent price appreciation for similar properties in the area?
- Are there any new developments in the area, such as highway or transit construction or a major new employer, that make this an appealing home for prospective tenants and that could eventually increase the value of the property?
- Is there a new tax assessment for the area, which could increase property taxes?

Here's a short anecdote. At one brand-new townhouse complex in Kitchener, I called the listing realtor to ask a few questions: How much would the townhomes rent for? What was the vacancy rate in the area? Did she know of any new employers coming into the area or of any other developments that would make the area better to live or invest in? She could not provide the answers, since she did not work with investors or people looking to buy properties to rent out. Her focus was purely on selling the units to buyers of primary homes, and she could talk only about upgrades and other features in the homes. Luckily for my client, he did not have to worry, as I knew the area well, and could help him look at the bigger picture.

It's an investor-savvy agent's job to gather this kind of information to help you, as an investor, make informed decisions on areas and properties to invest in, and to teach you what to look for on your own. They should know what's happening in the area over, say, the next five years. For example, are there any new construction, economic, or development projects planned or underway, such as upgrades to major highways or new transportation infrastructure? They should understand the demographics of the tenants the area attracts and have suggestions at hand to improve potential properties to make them more desirable than other competing rental properties. And they should offer ideas for your exit strategy—presumably resale in due course.

How to Get Good Comparables

As mentioned earlier, comparative market analyses (CMAs) or comparables are one of the most valuable services licensed agents can provide their clients. These reports include details on recent buying and selling activity in the neighbourhood, size and style of the property, how long each house was on the market, the asking and selling prices, and other critical information, which, as an investor, you can then use to guide your buying and selling decisions.

Getting accurate comparables can be challenging if you do not know your search criteria or the neighbourhood in question. It's quite common, for example, for two or three realtors to look at the same property and have different opinions on its value. That's why it's critical for you to see the CMA yourself, to see what the realtors base their opinions on and how they arrive at their estimated value.

Have you ever sold your home and asked three realtors for their opinion? It's the same house, but the three agents may come up with three completely different prices, and even more price range differentiation if the property needs work. The After Repair Value (ARV), what a property would be worth after improvements are made, is harder to estimate. To get the best ARV possible, you need to use both sold and listed comparables. You want to know how much the comparables listed and sold for because you need to know what people are willing to pay for the property based on the sold comparables (market value), and you need to know what your competition is doing when you put your property on the market to sell.

When looking for sold comparables, your search criteria should consist of the following:

- similar properties on the same street, or

- similar properties in the same area, or

- similar properties in the same town, if none of the above comparables is found (for more unique properties, you might need to search the whole town)

- a time frame of six months back, or three months in a hot market

- the same number of bedrooms and bathrooms as the subject property (if you are unable to find comparables with the same number of bedrooms and bathrooms, you can have a variance of one less bedroom and/or one less bathroom)

You can also search the history of the subject property, when it was last sold and how many times it has turned over.

Relying on your agent's years of experience and knowledge of the local housing market to interpret the data and make recommendations, you will compare the CMA information to the property you are considering purchasing. You must get a CMA for every property you are considering buying or selling, as this is the key way to determine the appropriate price.

TAHANI'S TIP

Never rely only on a realtor's opinion of a property. Always ask for their opinion, but also look at the comparables yourself.

DIFFERENCES BETWEEN REGULAR AND INVESTOR-SAVVY AGENTS

Consider some of the key ways investor-savvy realtors differ from their more generalist colleagues:

- **General-Purpose Realtor:** Thinks short-term about individual deals

- **Investor-Savvy Realtor:** Considers the long-term objectives of the investor and is focused on the long-term relationship, not one deal

- **General-Purpose Realtor:** Is focused on buying and selling houses

- **Investor-Savvy Realtor:** Pays constant attention to local developments and educates his or her clients accordingly

- **General-Purpose Realtor:** May not know much about local economic developments

- **Investor-Savvy Realtor:** Is always attuned to local economic developments and helps interpret what they mean to clients

- **General-Purpose Realtor:** Sells an investment property and calculates only the mortgage plus taxes, and if the rent exceeds that total, then considers it cash flow

- **Investor-Savvy Realtor:** Takes into account the mortgage, property taxes, land transfer taxes, inspection and appraisal fees, property management fees, vacancy fees, insurance, maintenance fees, legal fees, and all other operating expenses to determine whether a property can generate cash flow

- **General-Purpose Realtor:** Sells property based on price (for example, may encourage buyers to "invest" in Windsor because prices are cheap there)

- **Investor-Savvy Realtor:** Looks for and sells in areas with strong fundamentals, and would educate buyers about *why* prices are cheap in Windsor and will suggest other stronger areas to invest in

- **General-Purpose Realtor:** May sell all over a region or province in an attempt to make money, even though he or she doesn't really know the local market

- **Investor-Savvy Realtor:** Specializes in one area or town that he or she knows, and is an expert in that market

Indeed, an investor-savvy agent is a crucial part of your team—perhaps the most important member. As you grow your real estate holdings and acquire not just more properties but also experience and knowledge, you will gain some of the market assessment skills an agent excels in. You will be able to carry out more of your own due diligence on potential areas and properties. Your agent becomes almost a coach in this regard.

Make no mistake—as an investor, it's *your* money, so you must take ownership and responsibility and be fully invested in learning about the process and the key decision points in finding suitable areas and properties. But this is their *job*. This is what they specialize in. So, assuming you find the right investor-savvy agent, this expert knowledge and service they provide you is worth . . .

Well, remember at the beginning of the chapter I asked you, "How much would that be worth to you?" The short answer is that the expertise is invaluable. Indeed, it's difficult to put a price on such value, because it's not just about dollars and cents—it's also about confidence and peace of mind.

Think about it: while your investor-savvy agent is using his or her expertise to help you find and acquire your next investment property, what could you be doing with the time you'd be saving? How much money might you have saved by avoiding costly mistakes? If you're a full-time investor, you could focus on managing your business of existing properties and researching other potential purchases. If you're working at a full- or part-time job and investing on the side, it would allow you to manage your daily life—not just at work but also at home, with your partner, kids, or whatever other passions you may have.

What is *that* worth to you?

If you're serious about becoming a sophisticated real estate investor, the answer just might be "priceless."

TAHANI'S TOP 10 TIPS FOR SUCCESS

1. Connect with an investor-savvy agent.

2. Create specific goals.

3. Clearly define a strategy.

4. Understand that investing in real estate is not passive income; it actually requires work, time, and attention.

5. Recognize that it is a *business*, and must be treated like one.

6. Focus on the big picture and look for strong cash-flowing deals, rather than keep waiting for that one big deal.

7. Know that the work doesn't end once you find a property and put in an offer—the work must continue; the property and tenants must be maintained and managed. Think of it like a marriage: all the excitement comes at the beginning, but the real test comes after the honeymoon phase, when the couple has children and endures all the ups and downs of life.

8. Maintain realistic expectations, rather than be fooled by TV infomercials about how easy it is to become a millionaire through real estate investing with little or no work, knowledge, or effort.

9. Focus on understanding the fundamentals of your local market instead of listening to too many opinions or being easily swayed by new reports about the market going up or down.

10. Take informed action. Some investors suffer from analysis paralysis: they are caught in a cycle of constantly *learning*—attending seminar after seminar, reading book after book—and fail to ever *take action*. At the other end of the spectrum, some know *nothing* but are so excited to become real estate investors they buy property without thinking things through or doing proper research.

REALTORS TAKE NOTE

We've looked at the advantages of working with an investor-savvy agent, so let's take a moment to consider the other side of the equation—the advantages of working with investors. Investors are a different breed. Few realtors are enthusiastic about working with investors. For realtors who want to understand how to work with investors, this can be quite a lucrative business. But one thing is certain: you need a respectful, trusting relationship where both sides get out of it what they are looking for—and that is success and profit. This really is the bottom line. Investors are numbers oriented; they aren't too concerned with or emotionally attached to properties, their curb appeal, the colour on the walls, or even their condition, especially if they intend to renovate and resell.

BENEFITS FOR REALTORS

1. Investors are repeat customers. For any realtor, this is a great advantage. Investors are often repeat clients within a year, whereas the average homeowner may be a repeat customer an average of every seven years.

2. Investors are good sources of referrals to other investors, as well as friends, relatives, and other associates. Real estate is a hot and sexy topic, and most discussions happen during summer afternoon barbecues or evening get-togethers. Therefore, if an agent's service and knowledge are strong, they are going to get a lot of referrals.

3. Investors are not picky buyers who want you to cart them around in your car all day. They are serious business owners. Most have full-time jobs and, therefore, only go out to see properties if the numbers work and they are serious about buying.

4. Investors are easy to work with. Yes, this may come as a shock, but once an agent and an investor establish a strong relationship, finding and completing profitable deals becomes an easy and repetitive process. This is very different from buying and selling primary homes, where the client and the process can differ every time. Investors can either search online for properties or use a realtor-provided list of homes from the MLS®, and they can drive by and view the properties themselves. Although dealing with novice investors is a lot of work at the beginning, investors can actually save realtors time, headaches, and frustration because they have a clear picture of what they want and what their goals are. Most investors are active, and once you explain the process and they understand the area and the numbers, and trust is built, most become easy to work with. The more deals one investor buys, the easier a realtor's business and life become. A realtor who finds good deals will have investors continually showing up, coming back for more.

5. Investors are usually pre-approved for mortgages or they know where they stand financially. Most investors know their numbers,

how much money they have to work with, and when they are ready to move forward. Realtors can walk first-time investors through the process with a savvy mortgage broker.

6. Investors don't usually ask agents to reduce their commission. They believe in the benefits and value an investor-savvy agent delivers, and they are usually happy to pay for that expertise.

7. Investors often purchase property when buyers of primary homes do not—such as during slow markets, summertime, or the holiday season—and whenever a good opportunity arises. Investors know that there are opportunities out there when the market is slow and people need to sell.

8. Realtors can spend less money on advertising, which is their highest expense. If they can reduce those costs by working with investors who have clearer ideas of what they want as opposed to advertising regular resale listings to primary home buyers, then that means more profit for them. If a realtor can find one serious investor who buys two or three properties from them in one year, that means lower costs for advertising, more commissions, and a more profitable business.

9. It is a competitive advantage for a realtor to become a specialist in a niche market with less competition. For example, a realtor within the Toronto Real Estate Board competes with 32,000 other agents, but for one who specializes in working with real estate investors, the number drops considerably. You may compete with only a few thousand other realtors, if not less. A bigger piece of the market means a more profitable business for these agents.

10. Realtors who themselves become investors end up looking after their financial health in a way that isn't taught in any real estate licence courses or industry seminars. If they buy only one income property, then they are better off financially than roughly half of the Canadian population. Buying one investment property a year, an agent can build personal long-term financial freedom while helping other investors.

It takes a special realtor to work with investors because these clients are very educated and knowledgeable about investment real estate. I present a two-day training workshop for agents who are interested in knowing more about how to work with investors. For more information, visit www. realestaterichesbook.com.

When the real estate market is slow, prices are low and listings are up. Investors typically go on a buying spree, since they may be able to acquire properties that are undervalued. Also, given recent changes to mortgage rules, young and first-time buyers of primary homes may find it more difficult to get into the market. This means they are likely to remain renters for longer than otherwise might have been the case, which is conducive to high demand for rental properties owned by investors.

Agents and investors who understand this reality and can work well together can build mutually beneficial relationships. Investors can acquire cash-flowing properties with strong potential for value appreciation—which means high profit. Realtors can establish solid relationships with investors that can enhance their careers and add real value to their bottom lines. Add to that the potential for repeat business and referrals, and agents can develop this part of their business to offset slowdowns in the resale residential real estate market, or replace it entirely.

GUEST COMMENTARY

How not using an investor-savvy agent can hurt you
By Dave Peniuk, Rev N You, Vancouver Island, B.C.

There is great need for investor-savvy agents in Canada. I say this from experience; we have struggled to find them in the markets we buy in. We do know of several in Canada, but unfortunately, we have yet to work with them because none are in our area.

Dozens of times, an investor-savvy agent would have helped us. For example, our first investment deal was accompanied by the advice of a realtor who said, "It's better if it costs you $100 a month anyway, because then you're not paying tax on the income." (In other words, the property would generate negative cash flow.) This is very bad advice, and thankfully not guidance we followed. Instead, we focused on getting a deal that would generate positive cash flow each month.

We have also had many deals that would have made perfect sense messed up by sellers' agents who didn't understand investors. If only they had taken the time to understand the benefits of a "vendor take-back" or "agreement for sale," they could have presented a compelling argument for our offer to their clients.

We have had to find our own way. We have worked with some agents with outstanding market knowledge who have helped us identify good deals. But ultimately, our investor-specific needs have had to be filled by our own persistence and persuasion.

An investor-savvy agent is such a huge advantage for a novice investor. Imagine having not only a coach who knows your market, the deals you're looking for, and what to do to secure the deal but also one whose success is tied to your success. In other words, the more good deals they find and help you negotiate, the more money they make. It's such a win-win situation and finding such an agent will make your real estate team stronger.

As a novice investor, if you find an investor-savvy agent, treat them like the gold they are. Never negotiate commission—they are worth every penny. Always send thank-you cards for every deal you do—or if you haven't yet done a deal, for every piece of advice they give you that makes a difference in your business. Build a strong and long-term relationship with that person, and you'll likely find yourself with the best and most lucrative deals in town.

GUEST COMMENTARY

How an investor-savvy realtor helps to add value to your property

By Brian Pulis, Pulis Investment Group, A Private Real Estate Investment Company, Toronto, Ont.

Our strategy is to focus on smaller multi-family properties (12 to 20 units), specializing in neglected properties. We recently completed several purchases where the existing cash flow was very poor. We encouraged the tenants to move out, then renovated the entire property and re-rented the units to a different tenant profile, at a 15 to 20 per cent increase. This approach created equity appreciation, as well as improved revenue.

Having an agent who understands our objectives is very important. We build relationships with our agents, educating them on what we're looking for—importantly, a property's marketability to our desired tenant profile. We have an agent in Barrie, Ontario, who really gets what we do and only brings us properties that fit our model. This year, he brought us eight deals; we purchased four of them and put offers on two others that we didn't end up following through on. With this focused approach, neither party wastes the other's time.

An investor-savvy agent also has potentially valuable connections. For example, this year we completed several deals that our agent brought to us before they were on the open market. It gave us a huge advantage in the negotiation stage. In the multi-family category, this is very common, so working with the right agent can be rewarding.

Novice investors take note: study the different categories within the rental market. I do this by first understanding the tenant profile I want to work with and then looking at areas and properties where these individuals want to live. Any work I do to the properties is designed to attract my desired tenant profile. If such tenants don't care to live in the area my building is, it wouldn't matter what improvements I made. Therefore, understanding tenant profiles, where they want to live, and what amenities they are looking for is critical. If your investor-savvy agent understands this process, he or she can be invaluable in helping you determine prospective areas and properties that will attract your tenant profile.

Your agent must do their homework to get a full understanding of your investment model. One who shows you everything that is currently listed without first determining what you're looking for is just wasting everyone's time. This was my experience when I began real estate investing, and I found it very troubling. I couldn't understand why my agent was showing me certain properties. As a novice investor who thought the agent was an expert, it totally confused me. The agent didn't have a clue how to explore different investment strategies, and therefore had no clue as to the properties that were worth looking at. Today, my investor-savvy agents are investors themselves, and they understand what it is we're trying to accomplish. They run the numbers on their own first before they consider showing me a property. They filter out properties that don't qualify, and thereby avoid wasting valuable time and energy.

If you find an investor-savvy agent you can work with, it's important to respect their time. Once they understand what you want, a great agent can then set out to locate it. They should then be rewarded with prompt follow-through from you. This relationship is very valuable, so if an agent spends time finding you a suitable property but you react with apprehension, they will pass those deals off to others who are ready to act.

2

How to Find an Investor-Savvy Agent

For novice real estate investors, finding an investor-savvy agent is a critical first step in building your team of trusted advisors. Choosing the right realtor can go a long way toward setting you on the right track in your career as an investor. With about 100,000 licensed realtors in Canada, there's one obvious question: How do you find one who is investor-savvy, who you're comfortable with, and who you can trust?

First of all, you want a full-time agent, as opposed to someone working in the industry casually or part-time. Not all licensed and registered agents practise real estate as their full-time profession. In fact, when the market is hot, many part-timers come out of the woodwork, trying to cash in on all the buying and selling activity for quick commissions. This is not the type of agent you want. You wouldn't use a part-time doctor, would you? Full-time agents must rely solely on their income from real estate, which means they are motivated to work harder for you.

You also want an agent who is active in the area you're buying in; there's no sense using a realtor in Ottawa—no matter how good he or she may be—if you're buying in Hamilton.

In addition to possessing solid local market knowledge (and being nice) you want a realtor who is an investor, has experience working with other investors, understands your strategy, can help you find positive cash-flowing properties to meet that strategy, can get the job done, and is a skilled negotiator.

But even narrowing the search with those criteria can be a challenge in some regions. For example, the Toronto Real Estate Board (Canada's largest real estate board) has more than 32,000 active members. If you are looking for property in the Greater Toronto Area, how do you go about finding the right agent for you?

The best way to begin your search is through referrals. Think about it: when you're looking for a trustworthy auto mechanic, a good dentist, or any other professional service, what do you do? You often ask your friends, family, and colleagues for recommendations of people they've used and are happy with. Do the same when looking for an investor-savvy agent. Ask other investors, your lawyer, mortgage broker, home inspectors, and other professionals involved in real estate.

THE POWER OF REFERRALS

From experience, I can attest to the importance of referrals. I'm a realtor who specializes in working with investors, and referrals are how I get most of my business. When clients are so happy with my services that they recommend me to other investors, it's very powerful and very rewarding. It may sound cliché to say that you can't buy such endorsements, but it's true. They really do speak volumes.

Begin your search for an investor-savvy agent by speaking to other investors about who they would recommend in your target buying area. Because real estate involves the purchase of physical assets, many of these investors will be able to show you tangible results to support their referral—strong, positive cash-flowing properties that their agent helped find.

NETWORKING AND CONTACTS

Look for agents who make networking a regular part of their business. Attending meetings of investment clubs, such as the Real Estate Investment Network, and of other business and community organizations, such as the local business improvement association, economic development board, chamber of commerce, city council, or municipal committees, is a sign that they take the business seriously. It shows they are keen to learn about new developments in their territory and any changes in the housing and mortgage industries that their clients need to know. Having a large network of contacts also means they will likely be able to recommend other members for your team, such as a mortgage broker, lawyer, or contractor.

You may consider joining a real estate investment club yourself. They can be an excellent place to meet like-minded investors who were once novice investors themselves, and they will be a first-rate source of information and referrals to help you make your agent selection. These clubs are also a good place to meet prospective agents.

A note of caution: not all investment clubs operate with integrity, so be extremely careful and do your due diligence. Many networks are there to try to sell you something; they teach you parts of their program at an initial meeting, but what they really want is for you to buy their materials, sign up for expensive ongoing seminars, or invest in their joint venture projects or their own real estate developments—which may not even exist. A simple Internet search using the keywords "real estate investment club scams" will produce a number of links you may find interesting. Ask the executives and members of a prospective investment club a lot of questions, including ones about unhappy clients or lawsuits. If there's even a hint that they're not being completely co-operative and transparent, walk away.

CONDUCTING YOUR OWN SEARCH

If you're not sure about joining an investment club and don't have any referrals, you'll need to begin your search for a realtor another way. Get into the habit of looking on the Internet or in the local newspaper of your prospective investment area. Note which agents have experience in investment real estate, are advertising investment properties, and seem to be the leaders in their local market. Get out and visit a few open houses and practise meeting a few realtors and asking questions about their business and level of expertise.

However, be careful not to be overly influenced by marketing hype. Realty firms and realtors are experts at advertising and promotion—including *self*-promotion. After all, helping themselves stand out from the crowd is a critical part of their business. Many of the large firms, in particular, have "President's Clubs" or other similar achievement and ranking programs for their sales teams, which allow just about any agent to claim they are the "Top" or "Best" in this area or that category. That may well be true in many cases, and for your prospective agent, but don't go purely by unsubstantiated claims or flashy presentations. Ask for real proof of their sales track record, and best of all, references to other clients—*investors*—that you can speak to.

At this point in your search for an investor-savvy agent, you will likely become very enthused about taking this important step and you may be tempted to move quickly. But it's important that you take your time and ask the right questions to find the right agent. Don't get caught up in the excitement and enter an arrangement prematurely. There are many stories of new investors who jumped into a deal too early because of an overzealous realtor whose focus was on selling a property, not on meeting the longer-term objectives and strategy of the buyer.

Remember, you're looking for guidance and expertise from your investor-savvy agent—but it's still *your* deal. *You* are the CEO of your real estate investing business, and it's your responsibility to take control and be very serious about searching for an agent who has the specific qualities and traits you need.

You're surely familiar with that old real estate adage: location, location, location. Well, I'd like to offer up another one: relationships, relationships, relationships. This, I believe, is what differentiates a great realtor from an average one, and what helps deliver value to clients. Indeed, relationships, relationships, relationships is something of a personal motto for me. While many agents focus mostly on single transactions—helping someone find and buy a home—investor-savvy agents focus more on building and maintaining relationships. Investor-clients, after all, are often repeat buyers who buy and sell multiple properties in a year, compared to primary home buyers, who may buy and sell once every seven years. Managing these long-term relationships is key to becoming a successful investor-savvy agent.

Like any relationship, key ingredients for both parties are trust, respect, and integrity. Without those, you may complete a one-time deal, but you will not have the regular contact and referrals that stem from a healthy relationship.

I enter into a relationship with my clients thinking not only that I'm going to sell them a house but also that I'm trying to totally understand their goals and objectives. I want to understand why they want to invest in real estate, what their plan is, where they're at now and where they want to be, how they got here and why they want to get to the next level. This helps me understand them more as people as well as clients, and I am able to help them more.

They may come to me with a specific investment strategy in mind, but after talking with them I may learn their knowledge is not yet strong enough and they need to start with smaller steps to achieve their goals. I might advise them to take a different route than the one they were thinking of. But this only comes through building the relationship from the beginning, so they know I want what's best for them. I'm not thinking about only a single deal, but about their family, their lifestyle, what they want out of this investment, and the relationship we're building.

TAHANI'S TIPS

When searching for an investor-savvy agent, look for:

- full-time realtors

- agents who are real estate investors themselves

- experience in working with investors

- local market expertise and strong networking skills

- referrals from other investors

- competence

- patience

- enthusiasm

- creativity and marketing skills

- an understanding of investors' motives

- knowledge and understanding of a local market's fundamentals

- proven performance in their field, selling a minimum of 12 homes a year

And remember:

- Don't enter into an arrangement prematurely because of a "hot" recommended deal.

- Do your own due diligence and don't be swayed by marketing hype.

KEY CHARACTERISTICS

Many regular realtors who don't focus on investors lament when the market softens and their jobs become more difficult. They typically complain that conditions are "awful," "ugly," and "so tough." How could anyone buy property from someone with such a prevailing view? My approach is to inform people about what's happening in the market, to explain to them the differences in the market conditions, that it may be a "buyer's market" or a "seller's market," how it affects them, and even how they might benefit from it.

As an investor, it is important to work with an agent who truly understands different market conditions and how they may affect clients, positively or negatively. You can't just look at a challenging market as half-empty—you also have to look at it as half-full. Yes, it is important to be realistic. A buyer's market may make it more difficult for sellers, but that only means realtors and their clients have to be sharper and more creative, doing things that they might not do in a seller's market, such as staging a home, making sure the price is appropriate, and offering an incentive.

Investor-savvy agents know how to educate clients about market conditions and how to be flexible enough to address whatever challenges the market presents. Personally, I take the position that buyer's markets present wonderful opportunities—such as more listings to choose from and sellers who may be extremely motivated and willing to deal. Conversely, when market conditions favour sellers, it's important that your agent understands and communicates the potential implications for you and can still help you find the best opportunities, despite any challenges.

A lot of it really amounts to your agent having a positive and creative mindset. Many of my clients say this is one of my strengths as a realtor. For example, when I was starting out, I had the opportunity to work with the top realtor in the Cambridge area and learned a very important lesson. He told me that the winter holiday season is a very quiet time for the real estate business, with people away and taking time off. But instead of accepting that there was no business to be done, he impressed upon me that this was an opportunity; for those willing to work hard, there would be less competition and more work available.

I learned that I couldn't just go with the masses, that to be successful, I'd have to think differently than others and be more creative than the average agent. This is one of the most important lessons and philosophies that got me to where I am today. It's important to look at situations with a positive mindset and to work with a realtor and other team members who have a similar outlook.

SELECTING THE AGENT WHO'S RIGHT FOR YOU

Once you've narrowed your search to a select few agents who are used to working with investors, who have local market expertise, and who possess the other important characteristics you're looking for, it's time to select *the one*.

Remember, this person will be a key partner you will rely on for both their knowledge and their referrals for other members of your team. It's important that you take the time to meet and interview prospective agents until you find one you are comfortable with and with whom you can build a trusting relationship. And speaking of trust, trust your instincts. If you get an early feeling about someone—positive or negative—make note of it, and as you go through your interview process, revisit those notes to see if anything else about the agent corroborates those initial feelings.

Whether your list of prospective realtors came through referrals or other means, by this point you should have at least a basic understanding of their areas of expertise. For example, you should already know if they are active in your desired investment town and whether they work with investors. Now is the time to drill down further to learn more about your potential new partner. Treat the meeting as a real interview, and come prepared with a list of questions that will satisfy all your curiosities about this person—everything from their personality and outlook to the technical knowledge they need to have in order to complete real estate transactions.

Below is a list of the top 10 questions to ask prospective realtors, which you can modify as you see fit, depending on how much you know about the person before you actually meet.

1. Are you a real estate investor yourself?

The value of working with an agent who is also an investor is that they have walked the very journey you're about to embark on. Their experience as a realtor combined with their experience as an investor creates invaluable expertise for you to draw on. They will have been in your shoes at some point in the past, and drawing from those experiences they should be able to help you learn what to look for and what to watch out for as a novice investor. Ask them what they learned from being an investor, how well they did, and how they have grown as an investor and as a realtor. This guidance can help you avoid potentially costly mistakes that a less experienced realtor may not even recognize.

2. How long have you been a real estate agent and how long have you worked in the area I'm considering investing in?

You want to work with a realtor who has been in the business full-time and working with investors for a *minimum* of two years. Helping a new agent gain experience in the investment side of the business may be the humanitarian thing to do, but not at the expense of your investments. Conversely, a realtor who has been in the business for a long time, possibly nearing retirement or with a different specialty, may lack some of the drive and hunger to work hard for you.

Local market expertise is critical, so ask about their knowledge of economic fundamentals, new developments in the area, municipal government activities, how they determine the potential of one location versus another, the vacancy and rental rates for the area and property types you're considering, and the tenant profile for the neighbourhood.

Ultimately, you're looking to learn what they have to offer and how they can help your business.

3. How much of your business is based on working with investors?

Most realtors don't concentrate on investors, since they find the work more taxing than dealing with primary home buyers. They typically find investors to be a lot of work, more demanding, and generally harder to deal with.

Look for a realtor who works with investors for at least 10 per cent of their business. You want a realtor who is on top of the market and has an eye for a great investment.

4. What part of town do you focus on and what type of investment is your specialty?

Cities vary in size, of course, and in large areas most realtors tend to specialize in one part of town, though they certainly can and sometimes do buy and sell properties in others. Toronto, for example, has many areas and neighbourhoods, and you find realtors specialize in downtown, or the West End, or Scarborough, or the Beach area. Look for an agent who specializes in the area you're looking to buy in. Ask what type of investment real estate they focus on, with what strategy, and in what type of building. As they answer, ask follow-up questions that come to mind to help you learn more about their investment business and how successful they and their clients have been.

5. What process do you use to determine if a certain property is a good investment?

This is such a powerful question—what I call a $1 million question. How prospective agents answer is very telling as to whether they truly understand the important criteria investors use to find properties. Ask about how they calculate cash flow and what the cash flow is like for investment properties in the area. Do they understand return on investment, cap rate, and other investment concepts?

If, in response, they ask you what your criteria are, pay attention—that means they are really on the ball and are a knowledgeable and experienced agent. Why? Because they can't tell you what is a good investment property without first knowing something about your goals and objectives, and therefore your criteria. Watch for this one.

6. What investment and financing strategies are you most experienced with?

Ask if they understand what a vendor take-back is, or a lease-to-own. Inquire about other types of investment strategies they have used, whether they have been successful and why.

Agents who know investment real estate likely know all these strategies and more (we discuss strategies in detail later in the book). They may not focus on or even regularly use all of them, but they should be able to explain them to you and ultimately help you figure out which one is best for you to start with.

7. Do you have a network of other professionals (such as a lawyer, mortgage broker, accountant, property manager) that you can refer me to?

It is important to build a strong team of professionals to help guide you along the road to becoming a sophisticated real estate investor. Look for a realtor who is well connected and can refer you to the professionals you need. These other team members should also have experience in working with investors, so you and your realtor don't have to spend valuable time educating them about the process.

8. What do you expect from your investor-clients?

It's a powerful message when a realtor is able to tell you what kind of client they look for, and whether you fit the criteria. It demonstrates that this agent knows their target market and understands what they are looking for and what to expect from clients.

For me, basic expectations begin with showing up on time for scheduled meetings. It is so important. It shows respect and commitment to the realtor. I also look for decisiveness and consistency. After I clarify goals and objectives with a new client, I look for follow-through on their commitments. If you say you're going to do something—do it. If an investor wants to implement a buy, hold, and rent strategy, and then on the next property wants to try a lease-to-own, that tells me they're jumping from one strategy to another, always looking for the proverbial greener grass. And it tells me that they may not really understand real estate investing as a long-term proposition, that they may be looking for a quick payday. I look for investors who understand the different strategies and then, once I know their goals and objectives, we plan a course of action together to achieve them. We make a commitment to take action and follow through.

9. What is the best experience you have had working with investors?

Listen carefully to how the realtor answers this question—not just what they say, but how they say it. If they say all investors are the same, that they waste their time and make them run around and don't know what they are doing, then you know this is not the type of agent you want on your team. Not every investor is the same, and overgeneralizing indicates the realtor is not in control of what they do and not clear about what type of investors they attract—and want to attract. A bad experience with an investor once in a while is understandable. After all, some investors are better and more comfortable with the business than others. But if an agent talks about *every* experience with investors being negative, that says a lot about them, not the investors.

What you're hoping to hear is how the realtor helped investors, what kind of growth they experienced, and if the agent is willing to provide references so you can speak to these clients.

10. What is the worst experience you have had?

Ask about any conflicts or disagreements they've had with investors in the past, how they dealt with them, and what the outcome was. Let's face it, real estate investing can be difficult, and when you're dealing with someone's finances—not to mention different personality types—relationships can sometimes be tested. Look for signs that they have good coping and communication skills, and that they can be fair and open to compromise, rather than ending every relationship that encounters a rough patch.

These are excellent general questions that should start the conversation flowing, but they are also specific enough that the answers you get should give you a very good indication of a realtor's level of experience and expertise.

Whenever potential clients interview me, I welcome these types of questions. In fact, I am pleased to see someone taking the time to ask for such detailed information. It shows they are serious about their business and that our interests might align well.

If I meet with someone who hasn't yet taken the time to prepare in this way, I ask them to do it. I see that very first meeting as, potentially, the beginning of a relationship. And while I appreciate the fact that they have called me, I advise them that next time they should ask more questions and take the interview a little more seriously.

The more you can learn about a prospective agent, the better you will be able to decide whether to work with them. For example, if you get the sense that a realtor really doesn't have the level of experience in working with investors that you're looking for, or that they're likely to be too busy with another part of their business to give your relationship due attention, then you can use that information to help guide your decision.

The First Meeting

Generally speaking, a first meeting with a prospective agent should be about one hour long. That usually gives both parties enough time to get comfortable with each other and to sufficiently explore all areas.

It's a good sign if an agent is prepared and wants to know more about you as an investor, not just the other way around. Remember, this is a relationship, and the need for a good fit, trust, and understanding goes both ways.

Before I meet with clients for the first time, I send them a questionnaire to complete and return to me, so I can get a basic idea of their financial situation and their objectives as investors. In the same way that they need to understand more about me, and my background, I need to understand them.

We explore goal setting in more depth in Chapter 14, but in an initial meeting, it's important for a realtor to learn the basics of the investor's situation. What are their desires and what specific goals do they have in mind with their real estate investments? Where are they now, financially? Do they have a down payment, or where is the start-up money coming from?

We also discuss the various investment strategies that might be suitable for them, potential investment areas and towns, the different types of agency relationships, financing options, mortgage pre-approval, and, importantly, our basic mutual expectations.

Residential investment real estate is a very specialized field, so you should be able to fairly easily spot realtors who are inexperienced in this area—or who are stretching the truth regarding their experience. Remember the story I told you in Chapter 1 about the realtor who couldn't answer basic questions about investment real estate? Well, if you ask prospective agents similar questions, the depth and clarity of their answers should tell you pretty clearly how well informed and honest they are.

Is a neighbourhood you're considering to buy in attractive to renters? What is the recent price appreciation for properties in the area? What can properties rent for and to whom? Are there any new developments that make homes in the area appealing to prospective tenants and that could eventually lead to property value increases?

These are very specific questions, and a realtor who is experienced in investment real estate and in working with investors will have no trouble answering them. If a prospective agent gives fuzzy or unclear answers or says they need to get back to you on just about everything you ask them, that could indicate a lack of knowledge in investment real estate, or in the local area you're looking to buy in.

Watch out for an agent who tries to push you into an area, neighbourhood, or property that doesn't feel right. If you feel like you're being subjected to a "hard sell," that could indicate that the realtor may not have your best interests at heart, or may be acting as a dual agent without fully disclosing this to you (which they are legally obligated to do).

The Final Selection

Once your interview process has pared down your list of prospective agents to the one or two strongest candidates, go back and review all your notes and do a final check.

- Are they a full-time agent who knows investment real estate?

- Are they experienced in working with investors?

- Are they up to date on economic developments for your prospective investment town?

- Are they plugged in to the local business community and any networking sources for economic news?

- Do the investor references check out to your satisfaction?

- Are they adept at the technical parts of their job, such as preparing offers and negotiating hard on your behalf?

- Do you feel you can trust them?

- Do your personalities mesh?

- Are you satisfied that they will represent your best interests and will give your business due consideration?

- Do they have a strong network of professionals to whom they can refer you?

- Are they skilled at helping you market, operate, and eventually sell your property?

Asking and honestly answering these questions should give you the confidence to make the final selection from an informed and knowledgeable point of view. Remember, this is a business relationship, a partnership, you're entering into, so be sure you're choosing a realtor who provides you with a good combination of technical expertise, business acumen, and communication skills.

Take the time to choose the right realtor, and you will relish the decision throughout your career as a real estate investor. Rush it and make the wrong choice, and it could be a decision you come to regret, which could also cost you thousands of dollars.

GUEST COMMENTARY

Leveraging your relationship with your investor-savvy agent

By Wade Graham, Higher Ground Real Estate Investments Inc., Calgary, Alta.

I went through many realtors before I found an investor-savvy agent who knew what I was doing and understood the process. This realtor was investing in a similar way and got the fact that this is a numbers game and that I really don't care too much about things such as the carpet. This relationship is of great value to me as it saves both of us hours of hunting for property, and inevitably makes us money. We spend one day a month doing a tour and seldom do we end up at properties that are totally outside of my scope.

Novice investors should not waste time (your most valuable resource) working with agents who don't specialize in a specific area. If you're looking for multi-family, then don't work with an agent who specializes in single-family homes. Interview several agents and find one who works for you. This probably isn't the guy your dad used as an agent when he bought his house. You want an agent who is savvy in the investment world and isn't afraid to write offers and negotiate hard for you.

Some of my deals involve joint venture partners. Many of them are less experienced investors who come to me with cash, and are leveraging my knowledge and my relationships with others (such as my investor-savvy agent).

If you're considering a joint venture partnership, your prospective partners will want to see what your team looks like. If you're working with amateurs and a non-investor-savvy agent, this makes you look like an amateur.

Work with the best to be the best.

GUEST COMMENTARY

Hire slow, fire quick

By Mark Loeffler, The Versatile Investor, Toronto, Ont.

For novice investors, taking the time to find the right investor-savvy agent is one of your most important first steps, so don't rush it. You will be relying on their expertise and advice, especially in your first few deals, so it's important you make sure they have the experience and knowledge—as a realtor *and* as an investor—that you will need. In effect, you're looking for a business partner, not a friend, so be discerning in making sure they have the professional qualifications, as well as the people skills and personality traits that make you feel comfortable, and that will come in handy when it comes time to make a deal.

With tens of thousands of agents out there, and maybe hundreds if not thousands in your prospective investment area, networking with other real estate investors is the best way to find the right one for you. Get names and numbers and interview until you feel you have the right fit of credentials and skills that suit you.

When you first meet with prospective agents, find out where they are currently buying and what investment strategies they are implementing, either as investors themselves or on behalf of their clients. Go with a plan—if you are prepared, you will be able to more effectively tell your story, and this will help the agent understand your goals and objectives and how they can help you. To ensure you have an effective plan, know how much capital you have to invest by speaking to a mortgage broker who works with investors. People don't plan to fail, they fail to plan. The more information you have walking into a meeting, the more productive it will be.

Once you have found an agent, it is important to develop and maintain a healthy relationship. And make no mistake, it is a relationship, and communication is critical. Be honest and open about what you are looking for, but also be realistic; if your realtor really is good and you're taking up too much of their time or are otherwise "high maintenance," they may fire you. Good agents are busy and don't hesitate to fire clients who are time-wasters. On the other hand, if an agent is showing you properties that don't meet your strategy, you should let them know. It works both ways: if they are wasting your time, fire them and move on.

Hire slow, fire quick.

3 Types of Agent Representation

If you've chosen the agent you'd like to work with, congratulations! But you're not quite ready to head out and view properties. You still need to determine what type of representation you are going to require and whether you're going to formalize it with a signed agreement. Real estate agency relationships and representation have been a hot topic over the last couple of years. No longer is it as simple as buyer's, seller's, or dual representation. Increasingly, there are agencies offering discount services, as well as "for sale by owner" groups, which focus on helping homeowners sell their properties with lower fees than those normally associated with sales through full-service brokerages.

CHANGING LANDSCAPE

This issue was prominent news throughout 2010, as the Competition Bureau, an independent federal law enforcement agency whose mandate is to ensure Canadian businesses and consumers prosper in a competitive and innovative marketplace, took on the Canadian Real Estate Association (CREA). The bureau contended that CREA's Multiple Listing Service (MLS®) was an anti-competitive home-listings system that artificially increased the cost of real estate transactions.

Owned by CREA, which represents about 100,000 members at approximately 100 real estate boards across Canada, the MLS® is an Internet-based system that lists properties for sale. An estimated 90 per cent of all residential real estate transactions in Canada involve the MLS®.

In February 2010, following three years of discussions and several months of negotiations, Commissioner of Competition Melanie Aitken officially challenged the "anti-competitive rules imposed by CREA on real estate agents who list residential properties using the Multiple Listing Service system."

The bureau asserted that consumers should have the option of choosing real estate services on an à la carte basis, rather than only being offered full-service packages and full-rate fees. The current practice, the organization said, was a way of limiting competition.

CREA, on the other hand, sought to protect the MLS®. It had become an invaluable tool for realtors, and helped them generate billions of dollars in commissions. Under the existing structure, the industry could tightly control the MLS® listings and ensure their accuracy.

For consumers, a deregulated system might produce more competition for their business, if more companies were to offer cut-rate services. Those who wanted minimal interaction with an agent would still be able to list their homes on the MLS®, to guarantee wide exposure.

After months of well-publicized debate, the bureau announced on September 30, 2010, that it had reached a 10-year agreement that fully resolved the commissioner's concerns. CREA and its members endorsed the deal.

Under the agreement, CREA was to eliminate its anti-competitive rules, including those that discriminate against real estate agents who are hired by consumers to offer a "mere posting" service. In the case of mere postings, a seller hires a real estate agent only to list a property on the MLS® system and agrees to handle all other details of the transaction directly.

"This resolution is welcome news for both consumers and real estate agents in Canada," Aitken said in announcing the deal. "For Canadian homeowners, it ensures that they will have the freedom to choose which services they want from a real estate agent and to pay for only those services. For real estate agents, it ensures that they will be able to offer the variety of services and prices that meet the needs of consumers."

With all the attention brought on the industry as a result of the Competition Bureau's challenge, CREA has stepped up efforts to communicate and market its services and the value its members offer to Canadian home buyers and sellers.

What Does the Settlement Mean for Canadians?

When CREA and its nearly 100,000 members voted to endorse the agreement, the issue caught the attention of homeowners and prospective home buyers and sellers because, at its root, it centred on them potentially saving thousands of dollars in real estate commissions. At the same time, it could be argued that many Canadian consumers didn't fully understand the matter, let alone know how the change might really affect them.

One of the benefits of the agreement, for consumers as well as CREA, was that it ultimately would protect the integrity of the data on the MLS®, since any listings would still have to be posted by a licensed real estate agent. Some thought it might also lead to new business models with varying structures and fees for real estate services, which, in theory at least, could offer consumers savings on commission fees.

Among the other possible impacts:

Polarization in the profession: Experienced, professional realtors who provide full and value-added services with expertise and excellence will continue to find clients for their businesses, even if they do have to work harder. Meanwhile, discount brokerages and those offering à la carte services may appeal to some consumers, but for how long? People may well learn that it's not as easy to sell houses on their own as they first thought, and they may have to rely on their lawyers (to whom, of course, they would pay more in legal fees) to review and complete transactions.

A void in real services: In soft markets, realtor expertise and know-how can be the difference between a home that sells quickly and at fair value, and one that languishes on the market and must eventually be reduced in price.

An "artificial" market: If sellers can list their homes for relatively low costs and with virtually no commitment, this could lead to a groundswell of new listings or to more homes listed by owners who may not be seriously interested in selling but are just testing the waters. This could, in turn, lead to or exacerbate soft market conditions.

Increased out-of-pocket expenses for sellers: By selling their home through a discount brokerage, sellers may be able to avoid paying full-service seller's agent fees. But then they themselves are on the hook for upfront costs for things such as advertising. And if a buyer comes via a licensed realtor, the seller will likely still have to pay that buyer's agent a commission.

No way to qualify buyers: One of the intangible services that realtors provide is qualifying prospective buyers—separating the seriously interested from the tire kickers. Under the new system, sellers could waste untold hours scheduling viewings and open houses for people who are not serious buyers or who are otherwise not qualified. Bottom line? Potentially, lots of wasted time.

These are just some of the potential impacts of the new system, which, in theory, could still lead to a more competitive market and more choices for Canadian consumers, which can be a good thing.

In practice, however, things may prove a bit more challenging.

In May 2011, for example, one brokerage opened for business in Ontario, promising to "shake up commission rates" in the province. One Percent Realty Ltd. Brokerage, originally launched in Newfoundland, expanded into Toronto and Ottawa. The company charges 1 per cent plus $900, with a $9,600 minimum (instead of the usual 5 per cent), to sell a house, and One Percent then shares that commission with the buyer's agent.

While drastically reduced commissions may sound like music to sellers' ears, there are those who believe that approaches such as One Percent's make great marketing slogans, but don't offer a sustainable business model. Critics argue that it's unlikely a realty firm with such a low fee structure could realistically provide valuable services to many clients for any length of time—meaning it is the type of brokerage that may appeal only to a very narrow market segment, and possibly only during a best-of-times sellers' market.

COMPETITION BUREAU TO SUE TORONTO REAL ESTATE BOARD

Just when you thought you might be starting to understand the war between the Competition Bureau and the realty industry, the bureau announced it is waging another battle—this one against the country's largest real estate board.

On May 27, 2011, the Competition Bureau filed an application with the Competition Tribunal seeking to prohibit anti-competitive practices by the Toronto Real Estate Board (TREB). These practices are alleged to deny consumer choice and restrict how approximately 32,000 TREB member agents can provide information from the Toronto MLS® system to their customers, thereby denying member agents the ability to provide innovative brokerage services over the Internet.

"Today, consumers are demanding a greater selection of service and pricing options when buying or selling their homes and many agents are eager to accommodate them," Melanie Aitken, commissioner of competition, said in a press release. "Yet TREB's leadership continues to impose anti-competitive restrictions on its members that deny consumer choice and stifle innovation."

TREB controls the Toronto MLS® information and only members have access to more detailed information than what is available on public sites such as www.realtor.ca. For example, the Toronto MLS® system contains data about previous listing and sale prices, historical prices for comparable properties in the area, and the amount of time a property has been on the market. The bureau alleges that TREB is preventing agents from sharing this kind of information with clients through such means as password-protected websites; therefore, it is seeking a legally binding order from the tribunal to ensure "greater competition and increased innovation in the market for real estate services in Toronto and the surrounding area."

TREB, naturally, disagrees with the Competition Bureau's position.

"TREB strongly believes in open competition and has taken numerous steps to empower realtor members in their Internet use," Toronto Real Estate Board president Bill Johnston said in a statement in response to the bureau's action.

I include this information here because you have likely been hearing a lot about it over the last several months and, judging by the TREB example, may continue to hear about it for months to come. It's affecting the industry, so it's important that we include it in discussions about realtors' services.

Naturally, 1 per cent commissions and other promises from discount brokerages will appeal to some Canadian homeowners and maybe even investors. But as you can see, this issue is a lot more complicated than many people realize.

TYPES OF REPRESENTATION

Even with increasingly tiered levels of realty services, there are still some basic common types of representation. While a signed agreement isn't required to formalize your agent representation, it can be beneficial. In fact, the Real Estate Council of Ontario (RECO), a public agency whose goal is to protect consumers and regulate the realty industry, requires that realtors ask their clients to sign a written representation agreement at the earliest possible time in their working relationship. RECO's Code of Ethics also requires that salespeople present a written buyer representation agreement for signature prior to the buyer presenting any offer. This protects the buyer from unscrupulous persons who may be posing as licensed realtors. (For samples of various agreements, see www.realestateriches book.com. These forms are typically full of legalese, so it's always a good idea to have your agent explain them to you in detail and to have your lawyer review them.)

Buyer Representation

A buyer's representation agreement specifies the services the brokerage will provide to you as the client. It's important to understand that this is a contract between the realtor and the buyer—specifically, the *brokerage* and the buyer, not the agent and the buyer. So, if you sign an agreement with a realtor at RE/MAX, for instance, and your realtor leaves the company before you buy a property, your agreement with RE/MAX still stands. However, the brokerage can release the agreement to the agent, if it so chooses. If it doesn't, the brokerage will try to connect you with one of its other agents.

Two types of buyer's agreement exist:

- a buyer representation agreement, which is suitable for clients looking for full realty services

- a buyer customer service agreement, which is suitable for clients who prefer to use the agent for only certain, limited services

The buyer representation agreement confirms that, for a designated period of time, the buyer has engaged a specific realtor firm to work on their behalf at finding a property. It also confirms the realtor's commitment to provide their best efforts to the buyer.

Essentially, such agreements signal the beginning of a relationship and spell out each member's expectations and deliverables. (This can come in handy if there are any disputes in the future over services or fees.) For example, the agreement:

- gives the real estate company permission to act on the buyer's behalf to purchase a property

- ensures full disclosure of all property information known to the brokerage. (This protects the buyer, because the brokerage can be held accountable if the buyer finds a fault or defect in the property after purchase and it is proven that the brokerage knew about it but didn't disclose it. For example, if I am aware of soil contamination in a certain area where you're planning to buy a property, I have to disclose this information to you. Similarly, if I know there was a death in a home prior to your interest in it, or that it was used for a marijuana grow operation, I must disclose this information to you.)

- spells out the time frame for which the contract is valid, usually less than six months

- specifies the geographic area where the agreement is valid and the buyer wishes to purchase property

- states that the buyer has not signed a similar contract with another real estate company

- sets out the commission structure for the process. (This section can protect the buyer, because it clarifies how much the agent is to be paid and by whom. If, for example, the commission paid by the seller is less than what the buyer agreed to pay their agent, the buyer is responsible for the difference.)

A buyer's agreement also affords the buyer certain confidentiality protections. For example, if a buyer tells me he's going through a divorce or is enduring other personal circumstances that may influence the timing or price of a deal, I have to respect his wishes for confidentiality. If I were to disclose that information to a seller against my client's wishes or without his knowledge, the seller could use that against us in negotiation.

This works the other way, too. If the sellers are going through a divorce and must sell quickly, it's my job to tell my client that information if I learn of it. The seller, though, doesn't have to disclose such information, and their agent *shouldn't* disclose it. If the seller's agent reveals such information—which could indicate *they* need the sale as much as the sellers themselves—they're opening themselves up to legal action.

A buyer's agreement can be established for a certain time period or only for a specific property that a buyer wants. Personally, I prefer not to work with someone who puts narrow limitations on the agreement. I view this as a relationship, and loyalty is important. If I commit to finding you a property, it may take longer than we both expect, but I will remain committed to the search until we succeed. I expect the same commitment in return. Some realtors, in fact, won't work with anyone who doesn't want to sign a buyer's agreement.

Keep in mind that if you sign an agency agreement with a realtor and a problem arises (for example, if you feel you are being neglected as a client or you are otherwise dissatisfied), you can seek to terminate the agreement. One way to accomplish this is an inclusion that if a conflict arises, you give the realtor a chance to correct it, and if that doesn't work, then you can end the agreement.

In the context of working with investors, there are exceptions to some of the situations described above. For example, if a client signs a buyer's representation agreement with me, and I spend a lot of time educating them about real estate investment, showing them properties, and explaining how to find and execute good deals, and they end up buying a property from another agent—they can still honour my commission if they want to keep our relationship. I have come across this, and my client honoured the agreement and paid the 2.5 per cent commission owed to me.

On the other hand, if a client ends up finding and buying a for-sale-by-owner property that I didn't show them, I may not mind if I don't get paid. I know that, as an investor, he or she will buy properties frequently and the relationship is more about the long-term than just a single transaction.

Every realtor is different and sometimes, depending on the relationship, circumstances—and commissions—are negotiable.

BROKERAGE'S DUTIES UNDER A BUYER'S AGREEMENT

- loyalty, in terms of protecting the buyer's interests in negotiations at all times

- obeying lawful instructions

- providing full disclosure, in terms of knowledge of a property or area

- ensuring confidentiality of circumstances or personal identity (e.g., celebrities)

- accountability, for such tasks as handling deposit cheques

Seller Representation

This agreement, between the seller and the brokerage, spells out the services the brokerage will provide to the seller, how it will market and sell the property, and the fee/commission arrangements. There are two main functions of this agreement:

- It confirms that you are giving the real estate agent the authority to act on your behalf for the sale of a property and to find you a purchaser. The agreement sets out the terms and conditions of this agency relationship, the length of listing agreement, the commission rate, when and how the fee or commission is earned, and when and how it will be paid to the agent.

- The listing agreement sets out the details of the property being offered for sale, including civic and legal address, list price, size of property, legal description, number of bedrooms and bathrooms and their sizes, type of heating, age of the roof, and other details.

A seller's agreement also spells out the brokerage's duties and obligations to the seller. For example, if a seller is going through a divorce, the brokerage must respect the client's request for confidentiality. However, if the seller tells the brokerage that the roof on the house has a leak, and the brokerage is asked about it by a prospective buyer or their agent, the brokerage must disclose its knowledge of the situation.

BROKERAGE'S DUTIES UNDER A SELLER'S AGREEMENT

- telling the seller anything known about the buyer

- ensuring confidentiality

- providing fair, honest, and full disclosure of information about the house

- providing listings of other comparable properties

There are three types of listing agreements you may wish to consider when listing your property with a real estate agent: a non-exclusive listing, an exclusive listing, and the Multiple Listing Service (MLS®). A non-exclusive listing permits several realtors to market the property. The one who ultimately sells the property is compensated with a commission.

An exclusive listing means the seller gives the real estate agent an exclusive right to find a buyer for the property for a fixed period. If you are satisfied with the agent but haven't yet successfully found a buyer, you can extend the time. This is done when an agent has a buyer and wants to sell the property exclusively to eliminate competition.

The MLS® listing is a highly sophisticated computerized database that is available to all members of the real estate board who participate in the MLS®. For the seller, this gives the property far greater exposure, since it is open to all agents from any other brokerages within the MLS® system.

Note: Because the listing agreement is a binding legal contract, you should be cautious about signing it without fully understanding it. If in doubt, seek advice from your lawyer before you sign.

WHEN AN EXCLUSIVE OR MLS LISTING ENDS

Real estate investors should be wary of thinking they do not have to meet the terms of an exclusive or MLS® listing agreement if a sale is made after an exclusive listing expires. Many of these agreements provide for a holdover clause, which protects the realtor when a buyer and seller are introduced during the listing period, and then agree to sell the property after the listing period expires. In such cases, the realtor is still entitled to a commission. The holdover period can be as long as the parties negotiate it to be, but it generally runs somewhere between 60 days (for residential) and 180 days (for commercial) after the expiry of the listing period.

Multiple Representation

In some cases, one brokerage will represent both the buyer and the seller—and both parties have to agree, in writing. (This is also known as dual representation or a dual agency agreement.)

Note that we said *one brokerage*. This means one agent representing both the buyer and the seller—such as if a realtor has a property for sale, and through his marketing efforts also finds a potential buyer directly. Again, both the seller and buyer have to agree to this arrangement.

This dual representation can also be two agents—one representing the seller and the other acting on behalf of the buyer—from the same brokerage. It can also involve two different agents from two realtor offices with the same owner—such as a RE/MAX in Kitchener-Waterloo, and a RE/MAX in Cambridge, owned by the same broker of record.

BROKERAGE DUTIES UNDER A MULTIPLE REPRESENTATION AGREEMENT

- spelling out rights, duties, and limitations for both buyer and seller

- disclosing all information pertaining to the physical condition of property

- does not have to disclose motivation for either party, unless permission granted by that party in writing

- cannot disclose financial preferences of either party

> ### WARNING: MULTIPLE REPRESENTATION LEADS TO MORE DISPUTES
>
> While there may be some commission savings in using one broker, more legal disputes arise in circumstances where the buyer and seller are represented by one agent than when they are represented separately.

Customer Service

A real estate brokerage may provide services to buyers and sellers without entering into a buyer or seller representation agreement. This is called "customer service."

Under such arrangements, the brokerage can provide valuable services in a fair and honest manner. This relationship can be set out in a buyer or seller customer service agreement, stipulating the services to be provided, but that the brokerage does not represent the buyer or seller as a client.

Real estate negotiations are often complex and a brokerage may be providing representation and/or customer service to more than one seller or buyer. The brokerage will disclose these relationships to each buyer and seller.

An example of this representation is when, as a realtor, I have a signed buyer agency agreement and the buyer wants to buy a for-sale-by-owner property that is not listed on the MLS®. The owner of the property is representing himself, and I am representing the buyer. Therefore, I am providing customer service to the seller and the seller will sign a customer service agreement in case he or she wants to continue self-representation or use a lawyer or hire a seller's agent.

Should a buyer not want to sign a buyer's agency agreement, then they can agree to a customer service agreement.

Other examples of the different agreements can be seen at the website of the Real Estate Council of Ontario, www.reco.on.ca. Your lawyer can also explain these to you and advise which type of agreement might be best for you.

For Sale by Owner

For sale by owner (FSBO) involves homeowners selling property themselves, with the hope of avoiding sales commission costs. While it may sound like a great idea to be able to pocket cash that might otherwise have gone to realtor's fees—and the debate over tiered realty services may lead to increasing popularity of this technique for some sellers—FSBOs are not for everyone.

In fact, I wouldn't advise novice investors to choose this route—and not because I hate to lose the commission. Selling property requires time, energy, research, and expertise. There are plenty of examples of would-be FSBO sellers who price their home too aggressively, only to watch the property languish on the market. And this can cost you, not just financially in terms of carrying costs, but also in stress and time spent away from your family, day job, or pursuing other investment opportunities.

Code of Ethics

At the end of the day, working with a realtor provides buyers and sellers with the peace of mind that comes from working with professionals who are bound by a CREA Code of Ethics. Real estate agents are regulated by provincial government legislation, and agents have to successfully complete an approved real estate licensing course and renew their licences annually.

TAHANI'S TIP

Who's working for you? It is important that you understand who the realtor is working for. For example, both the seller and the buyer may each have their own agent, which means they each have a realtor who is working for them. Or, some buyers choose to contact the seller's agent directly. Under this arrangement, the realtor is working for the seller, and must do what is best for the seller, but may also provide valuable services to the buyer.

4

Maintaining a Healthy Relationship with Your Agent

As in any other important relationship, open communication is critical to maintaining a healthy relationship with your investor-savvy agent. Although you are the boss, the CEO of your own firm, and technically your realtor works for you, it's important to always be respectful and professional, and to operate and conduct yourself with integrity and honesty.

Successful investors view their agents and the other members of their team—including their tenants—as equals, not just people who are there to help them become more successful. Think about it: everyone likes to feel important and respected, so if you treat your team members with respect and dignity, they'll be more likely to work hard for you.

Even the smallest things, such as respecting times you've set up for meetings and phone calls and replying to messages and e-mails in a suitable time frame, can solidify your relationship. And, as we discussed earlier in the book, the best compliment you can give a realtor is referrals—if you're pleased with the service, tell other investors and potential clients.

I have clients who call me whenever they see a property they like, although I may not know they are actively looking. They ask me to help them with the purchase, to prepare an offer, and to guide them through the other important steps. That makes me feel wonderful, because it shows trust and commitment. I don't need to worry that they are using other agents. They value our relationship and the knowledge and expertise I provide. They trust me and always come back to me.

TAHANI'S TOP 3 TIPS FOR MAINTAINING A HEALTHY RELATIONSHIP WITH YOUR AGENT

1. Hold regular meetings or phone conversations, with appropriate frequency to where you are in the deal. If you're not actively working on a deal, meet at least once a year, and consider treating your agent to lunch or a coffee so you can catch up and keep the relationship going. Each case is different, but you can judge for yourself what is good for you and your situation.

2. Celebrate your successes with your agent by sending a card, going to lunch, or buying them a small gift. The gesture will make your agent feel appreciated, and they will want to work even harder for you.

3. Provide referrals. Many agents' business cards include a phrase that goes like this: "The best compliment you can give me is a referral." It is so true in our business—in many businesses, in fact. If you're pleased with your agent, be sure to refer them to other prospective investors. Your agent will always appreciate your business, but will appreciate you that little bit more for recommending him or her, and it will help strengthen your relationship. Some clients may worry that if they refer their realtor to someone else, they will lose that realtor's attention, and that there may not be enough good deals to go around, but they don't need to be concerned: there are always enough good deals for savvy investors.

SHOULD YOU ASSUME YOUR AGENT IS ALWAYS WORKING FOR YOU?

How much should you count on your investor-savvy realtor to be working for you, whether it's helping you identify and stay on top of economic fundamentals or assisting you through the other steps involved in becoming a sophisticated real estate investor?

Remember, you are the CEO of your own company, and while your agent should be there for guidance and leadership, particularly at the beginning, ultimately *you* are in charge. Don't assume that your agent is going to be absolutely on top of every new economic development in your investment town. You have to take an active role in finding properties and becoming knowledgeable about what's going on in your investment area. Don't expect your agent to do all the work—*you* have to be involved. It's *your* responsibility to research and do your due diligence on prospective investment towns and properties, and for virtually every other step in the process of becoming a sophisticated investor. That is, after all, one of the key reasons you're reading *Real Estate Riches*—to learn more about real estate investing yourself, and to take charge of your own destiny in your new investment career.

Don't assume your agent is going to be constantly thinking of you and your aspirations. After all, agents are business people, too, and they have other clients and likely their own real estate investments to look after. If you're a new client looking to buy your first investment property and your agent has several long-term clients with multiple units, whose business is naturally going to command more attention?

If you do your homework and follow all the steps to find and choose the best investor-savvy agent for you, then you'll quite likely have a strong relationship with your realtor and they could well be doing everything they can to please you as a client. But don't automatically assume that's the case. *You* should take the lead and schedule meetings or telephone follow-ups, as necessary, depending on what stage you're at in acquiring a property. And always, always, always communicate clearly about everything, especially your expectations.

You can manage relationships with the other members of your team—your mortgage broker, lawyer, accountant, property manager—through contact as needed, but it's good to schedule a face-to-face meeting or business lunch at least once a year. When you're in the beginning stages of your real estate career, your interaction with these team members will likely be more frequent. But once you have purchased a rental unit and have been operating it for a while, your communication will naturally taper off and happen more on an as-needed basis. At the very least, you should get an informal annual report from them, but depending on the situation, you can request more frequent regular reports. Ultimately, you want to know how well a property is performing and if there are any issues that need your attention. A combination of communication methods, such as e-mail, phone calls, and meetings as needed, will help keep you informed.

AVOIDING CONFLICT

Human relations being what they are, even with trust and mutual respect, sometimes issues can arise. Open and honest communication, and both parties being realistic in their expectations from the very beginning, can go a long way to avoiding conflict.

For example, what if something happens in the middle of a deal and we're not happy with our relationship—then what? I tell people: if you don't bring it up, I bring it up. I ask them to let me know right away if something comes up, and if there's a chance I can fix it, I will try. But if I can't fix it, or if it's beyond my control, I will tell them that as well.

No one wants to be in a relationship where both parties are unhappy. If one of my clients is unhappy, most likely I will be, too; and if we can't somehow come to a resolution, then maybe we're best to leave things as is and part ways. There is no sense making people do something they're not happy with. Even if you're under contract, I wouldn't feel it's a win-win situation and there wouldn't be any sense in carrying on.

For example, I had one client who was a very detailed and meticulous investor. He wanted to proceed on one particular purchase, and I told him that if he wanted to go ahead, I wouldn't work with him on it, and I cited the reasons why. We both realized that it would be best to part ways, because he wanted someone attentive only to him, 24/7, and I couldn't do that.

It's important for both the agent and the investor to be open, honest, and realistic from the outset. You may not always be able to avoid difficulties, but you should remain respectful and professional no matter what the circumstances.

Common Frustrations

This is a two-way relationship, even though your agent technically will be working for you, and they will earn commissions from properties bought and sold. As with any relationship, frustrations will occur.

Good realtors, particularly ones who specialize in working with investors, are busy and in demand. Indeed, good realtors will qualify prospective clients—making sure they have the necessary funds, for example, to set out as real estate investors—in order to avoid wasting each other's time, as well as that of property sellers and their agents. Investors, on the other hand, want to know that potential agents have the necessary knowledge and experience to work with investor-clients. They want to ensure that the person helping them guide their real estate investments is qualified to do so.

Given these respective positions, then, it's no surprise that frustrations sometimes arise on both sides, when one party doesn't feel the other is holding up their end of the deal.

Following are some examples of frustrations typically felt by investors and agents, and some tips on how they can be avoided.

Investor Frustrations

1. An agent doesn't have the necessary experience in working with investors.

    Note: The best way to avoid this issue is to ask about experience early on in your agent-screening process. It should be one of the first things you ask prospective realtors. Don't be afraid to ask for refer- ences, investors they've worked with in the past, so you can speak with them to verify any claims the agent makes.

2. A realtor is relatively new to the investment side of the business and, therefore, lacks true insight and knowledge into important factors such as the local economic fundamentals—and doesn't network with the right sources to get that information.

    Note: Again, your screening and interview process can go a long way to avoiding this issue before it ever arises. Speak to other investor-clients the agent has worked with, and ask for specific examples of insight or local market expertise that helped the investor find a good opportunity and make a wise investment decision. Buying and selling real estate for primary home buyers is a very different task than buying and selling property for investors, involving a completely different set of parameters. You should be able to tell early on in your initial conversation whether an agent really has a handle on this side of the business, or if they only hope to expand into it.

3. An agent doesn't return phone calls or answer e-mails promptly.

   Note: It is important to clarify expectations of things such as communication before you enter into an agreement with a realtor. You should respect the fact that an agent has other clients and responsibilities to look after, but you also should be able to count on satisfactory responses in due time.

Realtor Frustrations

1. Investors don't have a clear plan or strategy. They have the *desire* to invest in real estate, they want to live the lifestyle that comes from earning profits, they want to get rich quick—but they don't have a *plan* to accomplish any of that.

   Note: The lack of a plan or strategy is one of the main reasons novice investors fail in real estate, so it's critical that you truly understand what the different strategies are, how long each one takes, the respective pros and cons, and what you need to do to reach realistic goals. And as an investor, it's important that you be realistic. Investing in real estate is not a get-rich-quick proposition. You should be planning for long-term investments—five to seven years or longer—and it takes time and a well-thought-out strategy to achieve your objectives.

2. Investors have unrealistic strategies in mind. They may have learned about them on a late-night TV infomercial or taken a course from a U.S. real estate guru on "No money down deals!" that they want to apply in Canada. They develop completely erroneous expectations about becoming a millionaire in one year through real estate investing—with little or no money, knowledge, work, time, attention, or effort put into it.

   Note: The old saying that "If something sounds too good to be true, it probably is," applies here. Late-night infomercials are famous for making things look unrealistically easy—whether it's the latest weight-loss gadget, the hottest new fabric cleanser, or in this case, the most lucrative overnight real estate scheme. Well, if it were that easy, everyone would be doing it. Part of your education in becoming a sophisticated investor is knowing that smart real estate investment does take work, time, knowledge, and, yes, money. But done properly, the payoff *can* be big.

3. Investors fail to understand that real estate investing is a business, and they must treat it like one. They incorrectly believe that the work is complete when they look at a property and put in an offer, when in fact the work is just beginning—from finding tenants to maintaining the property.

Note: In becoming a sophisticated real estate investor, you must look at the long-term big picture—including researching prospective investment areas and towns, selecting properties that will produce cash flow and appreciate in value over time, operating and maintaining the properties while you own them, and eventually divesting through whatever exit strategy you decide on. It really is like operating a business. You must conduct yourself like the CEO that you are, and manage your company accordingly every step of the way.

CASE STUDY: ALL HYPED UP WITH NO PLACE TO GO

I once had a lady named Jane call me. She said an investor she met at an investment club of some sort referred her to me. Jane said that she had taken a seminar to learn about investing in real estate and she was ready to begin her new career. She said she had already found a property on the market and just wanted me to help her prepare and submit an offer. The property was a multi-family building priced at more than $1 million.

In an e-mail to me, she said she was fully prepared and ready to buy, but had not yet been pre-approved by a mortgage broker, and that the down payment was coming from a joint venture (JV) partner. I sent her the questionnaire that I send to all clients before I begin to work with them, and I advised her that we would talk again once she returned the form to me.

Then, in a panic, she called my office and said it was urgent that she speak to me right away. She said she was interested in the property only if she could get a minimum 12 per cent cap rate (the percentage of return on an investment when purchased on an all-cash or free-and-clear basis). I also found out her partner had not really committed to a partnership with her, but had merely expressed interest in doing so. And that the partner had only $60,000 as a down payment, but she was looking at a $1.3 million property. Wow. At this point, my mind was reeling and I didn't know what to make of this "investor" and her ambitions as a real estate investor.

Do you see how leaping ahead while still an uneducated investor can lead to trouble? She has no down payment of her own, no JV contract in place, no clue about numbers, including what the market can give her in cap rate. And she wanted me to put in an offer right away without even viewing the property or getting real numbers—comparables, working through the finances. She was a graduate of a one-week seminar and all of a sudden felt she was a professional investor and ready to hit the jackpot.

Believe it or not, this is a common scenario. Immediately, I explained that this was not how I worked, and even if this was the deal of the century, I wouldn't put an offer on it until we both met and went over all the appropriate steps.

Unfortunately, facing these types of situations, some unsophisticated realtors hear the word "offer" and immediately begin running and spinning their wheels trying to pull off the deal to get their commission. But it is dead wrong. An educated and professional investor treats his or her business accordingly, working with a well-planned-out system that outlines both clear goals and objectives as well as the steps needed to achieve them.

Kudos to Jane, I suppose, for wanting to become a real estate investor and at least trying to educate herself to some degree. But one seminar does not a sophisticated investor make. As a novice investor, you must have the perspective and patience to truly learn about the business before you jump into the market, possibly with catastrophic consequences.

And for me as a realtor, luckily, I had the knowledge and experience to see right through Jane's overzealous—and unrealistic—ambitions, to know that it wasn't going to work, period. Any investor-savvy agent would have easily seen the red flags with such a plan, or lack thereof.

CASE STUDY: RIGHT IDEA, BUT UNREALISTIC EXPECTATIONS

An investor named Harry called me, saying he was looking for a realtor who knew how to find cash-flowing properties and specialized in my area—Kitchener-Waterloo and Cambridge. He said he would consider working with me only if I could find him properties that generate at least $800 per month positive cash flow, on properties of $200,000 to $250,000, and would only consider putting offers on homes that have motivated sellers.

I heard him out and then told him what he was looking for was amazing but that I couldn't find those properties—and that if he could, to let me know where and I would do a joint venture partnership with him! Well, okay, I am being sarcastic here. But if every $200,000 property could cash flow that well, then *everyone* would be buying and living on such investments.

Think about that for a second. Purchasing a $200,000 property with 20 per cent down would require a down payment of $40,000, leaving $160,000 to be mortgaged. With a 30-year amortization at 4.5 per cent, that means the monthly mortgage payment would be slightly more than $810. Let's round it up to $850 per month—which is conservative—to account for other carrying costs such as taxes, maintenance, and insurance. That means, to generate $800 in positive cash flow, the property would have to rent for $1,650 per month. How many properties do you think you could buy for as little as $200,000, yet rent for as much as $1,650 per month? I'm not saying it's impossible; such deals may be available—if you look long and hard enough and do your research.

The other problem with this scenario is that on the Multiple Listing Service (MLS®), the seller's agent usually doesn't disclose the motive for the sale—unless agreed to in writing by the seller, but this rarely happens. So, how could I, or any realtor, show him only properties with motivated sellers?

This showed me how unfamiliar with real estate investing and naive Harry was—he truly didn't understand how it works. Understanding a realtor's duties and what they can and can't do is important if you want to know how to work with your agent and how the realtor can help you.

Harry had the right idea about the importance of generating positive cash flow, but he lacked thorough knowledge about how to get there, and ultimately had unrealistic expectations.

There are, of course, other frustrations experienced by both investors and realtors, but these are among the more common ones. And while it may sound obvious, both parties having realistic expectations, conveying them clearly at the beginning of the relationship, and communicating openly and respectfully throughout will go a long way toward preventing issues from arising and toward resolving them if or when they do.

CAN I ASSUME MY AGENT ALWAYS REPRESENTS MY BEST INTERESTS?

Just as not all doctors, lawyers, mechanics, or even professional sports officials are created equal, the quality of realtors varies, too. Real estate is like any other business in that it can be very competitive, particularly when you consider the "product" you're dealing with—properties—typically cost hundreds of thousands of dollars, and the realtor commissions on the sale of real estate is in the tens of thousands. There are excellent real estate agents, and others who are not so good.

For proof of the latter, all you have to do is visit the website of the Real Estate Council of Ontario (www.reco.on.ca), or the equivalent in other provinces, and find stories like this one:

TRADING IN REAL ESTATE WITHOUT REGISTRATION LEADS TO JAIL

Aug. 24, 2010 (BARRIE, ON) – An Alliston man who traded in real estate without being registered and defrauded potential investors in the Barrie area of almost $90,000 was sentenced to 15 months in jail today and ordered to pay restitution.

Mr. X, who was wanted on a bench warrant after failing to appear on two similar charges in Mississauga last week, must also serve two years' probation beginning on the date of his release. Sentencing related to the Mississauga charges is pending.

Tim Snell, counsel for the Real Estate Council of Ontario (RECO), had asked that Mr. X receive a sentence of 18 to 20 months in jail.

The sentence follows a guilty plea in April to eight counts of trading in real estate while unregistered and eight counts of failing to deposit trust money. Mr. X formerly of Oro, Ont., had been charged in October 2008 with six offences under the Real Estate and Business Brokers Act, 2002 (REBBA 2002), but public response to the advisory posted on RECO's website led to additional complaints and charges.

Mr. X, who is not registered to trade in real estate in Ontario, had pleaded guilty to representing himself as a registered real estate salesperson and performing the services of a brokerage in real estate transactions. He also pleaded guilty to accepting trust deposits from consumers for real estate trades, and then failed to deposit the funds into a trust account as required under REBBA 2002.

"I think it's important to note that consumers were not able to recover their deposits because Mr. X was not registered," noted Mr. Snell, "and therefore, was not insured."

All registered real estate professionals in Ontario are required by law to participate in RECO's insurance program. Consumer deposit insurance offers protection in the event of fraud, insolvency or misappropriation of funds by a registrant.

Offences relating to REBBA 2002 and its regulations (other than the Code of Ethics) may be processed in accordance with the Provincial Offences Act. Individuals convicted of offences are subject to fines of up to $50,000 and/or prison terms of up to two years. Corporations are subject to fines of up to $250,000. Courts may also order convicted persons to pay compensation and make restitution.

Or this one, also from the Real Estate Council of Ontario:

FORMER REAL ESTATE BROKER SENTENCED TO YEAR IN JAIL

Charges laid under the Real Estate and Business Brokers Act 2002

Feb. 22, 2010 (TORONTO, ON) – A former Toronto real estate broker who misappropriated funds deposited to him in trust, was sentenced to a year in jail today. His brokerage was also fined $200,000.

Mr. Y pled guilty last November to eight counts of failing to ensure that while acting as a broker of record of Sample Realty Co., the brokerage complied with the Real Estate and Business Brokers Act, 2002 (REBBA 2002). The brokerage was also convicted of eight counts of failing to deposit trust money into a real estate trust account and depositing the money directly into a general account. For each of the eight counts, it received a fine of $20,000. A $40,000 victim surcharge fine, standard in such cases, was also levied.

The Real Estate Council of Ontario (RECO) began an investigation into [name deleted] and the brokerage in January 2009 after receiving a tip from an anonymous source about irregularities regarding a trust account.

After an initial investigation, RECO issued a freeze order, freezing the bank accounts of Sample Realty Co. The Registrar of RECO also ordered an immediate suspension of the registrations of Mr. Y and the brokerage, thus suspending their privilege to trade in real estate in Ontario and issued a proposal to revoke their registrations. On March 11, 2009, the proposal was upheld and both registrations were revoked.

The investigation by RECO found that on several occasions, beginning in the summer of 2007, Mr. Y had received funds from clients with respect to agreements of purchase and sale. The funds, to be deposited into a trust account, were instead deposited into the general account of the brokerage. Evidence presented to the court showed Mr. Y had signed deposit slips indicating funds had been deposited into trust accounts when they had not.

At the same time, there was a 10-month period where Mr. Y had authorized payments to himself from the general account totaling more than $120,000.

Though figures show consumer losses exceeded $133,000, they are not out of pocket due to RECO's consumer protection insurance. All brokers and salespersons must carry this insurance in order to be registered in Ontario.

RECO's counsel had asked the court for a one year sentence for Mr. Y. The maximum sentence allowed under REBBA 2002 is two years less a day per count. Mr. Y has appealed the one-year sentence.

These cases are perfect examples that not everyone in the realty business acts with honour, integrity, and honesty.

Remember, you are the CEO of your own real estate investment business, and given the amount of money—and your personal financial future—at stake, it's critical that you take managing it and your partners seriously.

From the very beginning, when you're first assembling your team of trusted advisers, make sure you do absolute due diligence on prospective team members, including your investor-savvy agent. Buyer's representation agreements protect you and ensure your best interests are being looked after, which is a good reason to seriously consider signing one. For more information on buyer's representation agreements, please see Chapter 3.

I don't mean to imply that all realtors are unscrupulous and that you should constantly be distrustful. There are many excellent agents out there, but sometimes, even with them, errors occur, either through oversight or honest mistakes.

The only person who really and truly always represents your best interests is *you*, and diligently managing your business and the relationships with your important team members is the best thing you can do for your real estate investments.

5

Expanding Your Team of Experts

Hopefully, you're now convinced of the power and value of having a strong investor-savvy agent on your team. And make no mistake—this is, in fact, *your* team. *You* are the CEO, and you make the decisions. These are your deals, your investments, your properties, and ultimately your financial future. It's important to assemble a team of strong professionals you feel confident in, comfortable with, and can trust. This chapter explains what each professional does and the fees they charge for their services.

Once you find people you can trust and work with, you'll never want to let them go!

THE PROS YOU NEED ON YOUR TEAM

The other important members on your real estate investment team include a real estate lawyer, banker or mortgage broker, accountant, insurance provider, and property manager. There will be other services you will require along the way, such as those provided by a home inspector and contractors, but these are the most important members you'll need on your team. It's advisable that they, like your agent, are experienced in dealing with investors.

MEMBERS OF YOUR TEAM

- real estate agent
- lawyer
- mortgage broker
- accountant
- insurance broker
- property manager

TAHANI'S TIP

With all team members, be clear about your expectations and communicate them in person and in a follow-up e-mail. This will help you to avoid conflicts later on.

GUEST COMMENTARY

Why my team is so valuable to me

By Ben Sanderson, DreamHome Today, Kitchener-Waterloo, Ont.

Not too long ago, I knew absolutely nothing about real estate. I certainly wasn't pouring money into it as an investment. When I decided to get involved in this business, one of the first great nuggets of wisdom I received was the importance of assembling a solid team of real estate professionals. The notion of surrounding myself with people smarter than me sounded a tad insulting at first, but it soon made a lot of sense. Why try to learn to do everything myself (an impossible task) when I could just get professionals to do it for me? That's exactly what I did, and it has paid off more than I ever could have hoped.

I asked other real estate investors I knew for recommendations. After a number of interviews and conversations, I had my team together—a mortgage broker, realtor, lawyer, insurance agent, and home inspector. They were all very familiar with the type of investing I was getting into—in this case, rent-to-own.

These people have proven invaluable in keeping me focused. Their encouragement and advice allowed me to purchase and fill seven single-family houses in my local area over the past year—about three times as many as I had hoped to be able to do. Knowing that you are backed by so much knowledge and experience helps to give you the confidence to go out and do things you otherwise likely wouldn't.

Each team member had a specific role. My realtor made sure each property I considered fit my specific investing criteria. This helped me avoid getting stuck with a house I couldn't fill with the kind of tenant I was looking for. My home inspector was great at helping me to understand minor versus major issues when buying a home, and ensured that each property I bought wouldn't have me paying for unexpected surprises down the road. My lawyer helped me not only with the purchase of each property (including some private sales) but also with making sure my rental documents were airtight, minimizing my liabilities and protecting my interests in the unfortunate event of an agreement going bad. To similar effect, my insurance agent made sure each property was protected with a policy specific to my needs as a rent-to-own investor. My mortgage broker may have made the most significant contribution to my success, and not just because he helped me finance these properties in a condensed time frame. Before I even began looking for houses, he took the time to discuss my five-year plan. Thanks to the insights gained from that conversation, he has laid a course that will steer me clear of many obstacles that might impede a lesser-informed investor. His guidance keeps me optimistic about what the future has in store.

One of the big misconceptions I had about real estate investing was that the money spent on a professional is just another expense. I now know how wrong I was. In truth, the money you spend on a competent professional who understands your goals is as much of an investment as any other asset you put your money into. Treat every transaction with your team as win-win and the successes you realize under their supervision (not to mention the expensive mistakes you'll avoid) can propel you further and faster toward your goals.

Lawyer

Real estate lawyers, you may find, specialize according to type of practice—such as condominium law or land development—rather than type of client, such as investors or principal residence purchasers. As you're starting out in your investing career, a good general real estate lawyer will likely be more than adequate for you. As you expand your business, you may need to become a little more selective in the type of lawyer you use. For example, one day you may find you need a lawyer who understands and has experience in joint venture partnerships or condo conversions.

GUEST COMMENTARY

Choose your lawyer—and assess their fees—carefully

By Shayle Rothman, lawyer and notary public, Parnes Rothman Real Estate Lawyers, Markham, Ont.

A real estate lawyer is not just a key member of your team; you are required by law to have such legal services to close your transaction. When selecting your lawyer, ensure they are a specialist in real estate and focus at least 90 per cent of their time closing real estate transactions. If you were to have laser eye surgery, you wouldn't go to your family doctor and you wouldn't go to your optometrist. You would research and hire a specialist who has completed thousands of laser eye surgeries and has a solid reputation. The same process should apply to your search for a real estate lawyer. Find a specialist for your *specific* transaction. Not every lawyer has the skill and expertise to close a real estate transaction and not every real estate lawyer has the expertise to close your specific property.

For example, the real estate lawyer you hired to close your family home may not have the experience necessary to close your multi-family, 15-unit, commercial property purchase. Whether you are buying three or fifty investment properties, you should follow the same rule when selecting a lawyer as part of your team: match the expertise to the required task. If you cannot find a real estate lawyer who has the expertise in both single-family and commercial/multi-family transactions (your preference should be to have one real estate lawyer, if possible, to handle all your dealings), you should employ two separate lawyers—one for your residential, single-family transactions and the other for your commercial/multi-family transactions.

The biggest mistake you can make is hiring a real estate lawyer based on price. As the saying goes: you get what you pay for. Find a lawyer who has competitive pricing, yes, but be sure to compare apples with apples. Real estate lawyers and the service they provide are *not* all the same. At the end of the day, your deal will close, but you want to make sure that you minimize your stress along the way and that your investment is protected.

As with the other important members of your team, when searching for a lawyer, referrals are important. Speak to your real estate agent, accountant, mortgage broker, and others for their recommendations, and make sure you contact and interview prospective lawyers *before* you retain their services. Your real estate lawyer should have experience dealing with your specific transaction, should be available to answer any of your questions prior to the closing date, and should meet with you to sign your closing documentation at no extra charge.

It's also important to make sure your lawyer is approved and authorized to close transactions electronically, as opposed to only through hard-copy documents, which can take longer and be more costly. They should also be an affiliate and registered with your bank, trust company, or lender, and be in good standing with the law society in your jurisdiction.

There are many costs associated with closing a real estate transaction—causing some people to cringe at the thought. Although you are required by law to have a real estate lawyer represent you for the closing of your transaction, it is a small price to pay to protect your asset that is likely valued in the hundreds of thousands of dollars. Make sure your lawyer provides you with a detailed written quote outlining the services to be provided.

Note: If it's not in writing it doesn't exist! You don't need surprises when investing in real estate. Your real estate lawyer is a key member of your team and you should not be second-guessing what the legal fees will be upon closing. Removing this uncertainty will only solidify your relationship with your lawyer, and give you confidence in knowing what costs you are facing. You should be able to call your lawyer to discuss any issues or concerns regarding your transaction without worrying about being charged by the second.

Where possible, request a flat-rate legal fee that includes internal disbursements such as title searches, couriers, and photocopying. Make sure you understand whether your legal fee includes disbursements or if they are in addition to the legal fee, otherwise you could be in for a big surprise on closing. Ask what third-party disbursements will be applicable, such as land transfer tax, title insurance, and government registration fees. This will assist you in budgeting your closing costs and ensuring that your legal expense is fixed and keeps you within budget.

For example, if you are closing a residential single-family transaction with a purchase price of less than $500,000, your legal fees, including internal disbursements, should be about $995 plus Harmonized Sales Tax, plus land transfer tax, title insurance, and government registration fees. If you are purchasing a commercial/multi-family property, the legal fee is usually based on an hourly rate plus disbursements, as each transaction is different. Speak to your real estate lawyer, as they may be able to provide a flat rate for such a transaction once they have a better idea of what services will be required. Commercial/multi-family transactions will always cost more than single-family transactions due to the additional expertise and documentation required.

Unfortunately, most people hire a real estate lawyer *after* the Agreement of Purchase and Sale has been finalized. Your lawyer should be consulted early in the process, especially if you are purchasing a commercial or multi-family property, since the documentation should be reviewed carefully to protect your interests. Your lawyer can assist you with the drafting of conditions, representations, and warranties along with clauses that require the seller to supply further documentation that may be essential to the closing of your transaction. There isn't much damage control your real estate lawyer can do once you have signed a firm and binding agreement.

Your lawyer should include in their quote the cost of reviewing/drafting the Agreement of Purchase and Sale, which is payable at the time of closing along with all other closing costs. If there are additional tasks, unforeseen at the time the quote was provided, that are absolutely necessary to close your transaction, your real estate lawyer should notify you in advance of such issue(s) and explain to you why the tasks have created additional costs. In these circumstances, your lawyer may only charge you their costs to handle such issues, or give you a discounted rate due to your relationship with their firm. This is why it is so important to build strong relationships with your real estate lawyer, just as with all of your team members.

Mortgage Broker

Mortgage brokers who have experience dealing with investors may be able to use this expertise in your favour with better mortgage rates or financing terms, and by helping you to leverage your money so you can buy more properties as you expand your holdings.

When financing a purchase for a primary home buyer, brokers, generally speaking, will go with a lender that provides the best interest rate for their client. However, brokers who understand real estate investing and have investors as clients will be able to do more for you. Since they see the whole picture, they will be able to source better terms for you from a credit union, trust company, private lender, or a bank, and will structure a better deal for you, whether you're working on your first or your seventh purchase. This will play a large role in your success, since you will hit your borrowing limit faster if you are only using a traditional bank. Once you are no longer able to use your income to qualify for more deals, your business will stop growing, perhaps at four or five properties or whatever your income allows you to buy. Working with an experienced mortgage broker will get you further by stretching your ability to buy more property, which in turn will make you more money.

When a new client contacts us, the first thing we do is send them a questionnaire to complete so we can get a basic understanding of their situation and goals. We then recommend they meet with a mortgage broker to get a pre-approval. This is important, as it gives both the client and us a clearer picture of their financial position and exactly how much buying power they have. If they need a broker, we can make recommendations, or if they already deal with someone, of course, they can continue that relationship. However, it's important that the broker they choose be investor-savvy.

GUEST COMMENTARY

A mortgage broker must focus on your portfolio, not just a single transaction

By Peter Kinch, president, Peter Kinch Mortgage Team, Dominion Lending Centres, Vancouver, B.C.

The process for arranging a mortgage for an investment property is different than it is for buying a primary home. The secret to success as a real estate investor is your ability to look at your mortgage as part of a portfolio—not a single transaction. The challenge for most investors is that the majority of bankers and brokers are focused on the transaction, as opposed to a portfolio. (An investor-savvy realtor also looks at your overall long-term goals, not just the purchase of a single property.) The impact of this on your future success can be significant.

Here's a good example:

I received a call from a client who wanted to purchase a rental property, and she had been working with a mortgage broker I knew. Following her conversation with the broker, her main focus was how she could improve the interest rate she was quoted. However, I quickly determined that interest rates were a back-burner issue. I started to ask about what her long-term goals were and why she was buying real estate in the first place. We discussed what results she was hoping to achieve over the next five years, and narrowed that down to determine exactly what results she needed from the properties she bought. As a result, we determined she would need a certain number of doors at $x a door to provide her with the cash flow necessary to live the life she wanted five years from now.

Once we established those numbers, we also realized she would not be able to accomplish all this with one lender. Since every lender has a "cap space" (the maximum number of properties or dollar amount they are willing to lend to one individual borrower), it is critical that her mortgages be structured in a strategic way to ensure that once she reached capacity at one lender, we already knew she qualified at the next. This can be achieved only if you have a plan and start with the end result in mind. This is the "portfolio approach." I simply play it out like a chess game. We never make a move without knowing what the next move is going to be. When a client works with a broker or banker who treats every mortgage as a simple transaction, they wake up one day and have hit the proverbial wall.

My client asked me for my best interest rate. The more appropriate question for her was: "How should I structure my business plan to accomplish my goal?" That is the difference between those who achieve success and those who are frustrated by the process. My client's goals were completely achievable, but her plan required the right strategy, and the order in which she chose her lenders was critical to her long-term success. Taking the time to discover those long-term goals was the key to being able to structure her mortgages properly and ensure she reached those goals.

Accountant

When you invest in real estate, how you position your company vis-à-vis the tax implications is an important topic that needs to be explored in depth. I recommend you seek out an accountant who knows real estate investing and is himself or herself an investor. Having the right accountant on your team can save you money, but more importantly, it will prevent you from making costly mistakes.

GUEST COMMENTARY

An experienced real estate accountant can save you time, money, and stress

By George E. Dube, Dube & Associates Chartered Accountants, LLP, Kitchener, Ont.

Why would investors want to work with an experienced real estate accountant who also invests in real estate?

Simple: investors will be able to sleep more peacefully at night knowing they will be taken care of—provided they are willing to listen to advice. If nothing else, you will know your accountant will be on top of the latest amendments to the constantly changing tax rules because they need to implement them in *their own* portfolio, and then yours will benefit as well.

We frequently acquire new clients not because their previous accountant was unqualified or unpleasant, but simply as a result of having a more comprehensive understanding of the industry and being able to speak the investor's language. Investors are often frustrated by having to explain the details of their real estate deals to their accountant—the person who is supposed to be the tax expert.

As an investor, select an experienced real estate accountant based on knowledge and expertise, as opposed to proximity. These days, with cellphones, e-mail, couriers, and other modern efficiencies, geography should be completely irrelevant.

Here are some ways a qualified real estate accountant can help you as an investor:

- more thorough understanding of the real estate industry and trends affecting it

- ability to plan for the next 10 to 20 years and on an intergenerational basis instead of planning for a couple of years; relevant real estate knowledge to help make appropriate structuring advice that is flexible and relevant for the future

- practical business and investment advice, which can earn or save you money, versus textbook advice

- having seen from experience what worked before and what didn't, can offer you practical advice

- can help Canada Revenue Agency auditors understand the different real estate plans and concepts, to demystify and professionalize your operations in the eyes of the auditor; can help ward off additional audit procedures when the CRA officials realize the techniques used were not only normal in the industry but also were used, in many cases, by the investor's own accountants

- save a lot of money and stress with proper initial structuring of your real estate business. (One example I learned of recently: an investor's business structuring, based on his accountant's advice, was not only poor from the outset, but incredibly expensive a few short years later. Business circumstances that should have been foreseen resulted in more than $55,000 in professional fees, plus a large income tax bill.)

Insurance Broker

Your insurance provider is a team member who is easy to overlook. Many novice investors underestimate the importance of insurance or fail to understand how one provider or package differs from another.

Make no mistake: whether you use an insurance broker or deal with an insurance company directly, having an investor-savvy insurance provider on your team is critical. Read on to find out why.

GUEST COMMENTARY

What real estate investors should know about insuring their investment property

By Philip G. Jarvie, HUB International Ontario Limited, Toronto, Ont.

Commercial policy versus residential policy: For their first couple of investment properties, many investors will add insurance coverage onto their existing homeowner's insurance policy. There are three concerns in doing this:

- Rental properties can become vacant. Residential insurance policies usually state that there is no coverage if the dwelling is vacant for more than 30 days, unless permission is granted by the insurer and a vacancy permit is issued. Usually, an additional premium is charged. Note that even if a vacancy permit has been issued by the insurer, damage caused by water escaping from the plumbing system or household appliances is not covered while the dwelling is vacant.

- Residential policies usually have a clause pertaining to the freezing of pipes. Essentially, they indicate that if the occupant is away for more than four consecutive days during the normal heating season, then there is no coverage for loss or damage caused by the freezing of pipes or by water that has escaped from pipes that had been frozen, unless the occupant had made arrangements for a competent person to enter the dwelling daily in order to ensure that heat was being maintained.

- Residential policies usually exclude damage caused deliberately by your tenants. Commercial insurance policies usually have much broader coverage with respect to tenant vandalism and water damage than residential policies. Even the vacancy limitation is usually less restrictive.

Important considerations to discuss with your insurance broker include the following:

Named perils coverage versus broad-form coverage: Named perils coverage or fire and extended perils coverage insure for causes of loss that are specifically listed and described in the insurance policy. For example, perils or causes of loss usually include fire, lightning, windstorm or hail, falling object, explosion, and vehicle impact. Damage caused by vandalism and certain types of water damage may or may not be covered, depending on the insurer. Broad-form coverage or all-risk coverage provides insurance against all causes of loss except those that the insurer specifically excludes. Broad-form is considered the more desirable approach.

Actual cash value versus replacement cost: This deals with how you will be paid following an insured loss. Actual cash value means that the amount that you will receive as compensation toward your claim will be based on the cost to replace or repair the property, minus an amount for depreciation. Depreciation will take into account the age and condition of the lost or damaged property. Replacement cost means that you will receive compensation on the basis of the cost to repair or replace the lost or damaged item without deduction for depreciation.

Coinsurance versus stated amount: Most insurance policies contain a coinsurance clause. Usually, there will be an 80 per cent, 90 per cent, or 100 per cent coinsurance clause. For example, a 90 per cent coinsurance clause means you must insure the property to at least 90 per cent of the replacement cost of the building. Failing to insure the building to that degree will result in you not being fully insured for the loss. You will end up paying a portion of the claim out of your own pocket (in addition to your deductible amount). Stated amount insurance requires that you sign and return a form known as a Statement of Values. This form will list the property values being insured. Once the insurer accepts this form, then the coinsurance clause is eliminated.

Rental income insurance: This coverage will pay for your loss of rental income if your tenant has vacated the premises due to an insured peril rendering the premises untenantable. For example, a fire or significant water damage claim could force your tenant to vacate the premises and therefore stop paying you rent. Your insurance policy would pay you for this loss of rental income until such time as the condition of the premises has been restored.

Sewer backup, flood, and earthquake: Not all insurance policies cover these types of losses, and you may need to specifically request this coverage.

Property Manager

One of the greatest challenges in assembling your team will be finding a great property manager. These professionals do more than just manage properties; they are also experts in their local markets, keeping up to date on vacancy rates, rental rates, and other important information pertaining to their area.

When a novice investor comes to me wanting to buy a property, one of the first questions I ask is how many hours they have available to put into it. Consider the following:

- Do you want to manage the property yourself?

- Do you want to use a professional property manager?

- Do you want to do—and are you capable of doing—any necessary repairs yourself, or will you need to hire skilled trades?

It's either time or money. If you can't or don't want to put in the time yourself, then you will have to hire a professional. When you own investment property, just like with your own home, there is always work to do—finding tenants, maintaining and repairing the property, shovelling snow, cutting the lawn . . . and someone has to do it. If not you, then who? And at what cost?

The answer to that question—in fact, most of your questions—should be determined by the fundamentals: selecting an area and property that suits your strategy and objectives, and how much time or money you want to put into it. Remember, the property you're buying is a business, and it's important to always look at it in that context. Cash flow is your goal, so if you invest $100 to repair or improve the property, what is that $100 investment going to get you as a return? How you're going to manage your business will help determine how much money it makes.

TAHANI'S TIP

Even if you decide to manage or maintain a property yourself, you must still include those costs in your calculation of running it as a business. Allocate a percentage for a property manager or maintenance person, so if and when the time comes that you decide to pay professionals for these services, the costs are already built in and will not eat into your cash flow.

The best advice I can give you is to interview a few prospective property managers. Communicate clearly and effectively what your expectations are, and follow up with an e-mail summarizing your meeting. Explain, for example, how often you would like to be contacted, what duties you expect them to perform, and other important matters. Ask them to explain their fee structure and how it might vary, for instance, if you, versus the property manager, find new tenants.

Don't be afraid to ask a lot of questions. A well-managed property is key to the success of your business; an improperly run unit—or worse, one that sits vacant for any length of time—can be very costly and damaging to your bottom line.

The following guest commentary includes some excellent questions to ask and things to look out for.

GUEST COMMENTARY

How choosing a property manager can save you money—and grief

By Adam Hoffman, www.hoffaco.com, Waterloo, Ont.

In selecting a property manager, a real estate investor should look to their trusted team members—realtor, lawyer, mortgage broker, and others—for referrals, as well as to local property management associations. Firms commonly vary widely on experience, services offered and, of course, price, so be prepared to spend a few hours performing due diligence by asking the following questions:

Do you take on properties in the area and of the type I own? Some firms will manage only single-family homes, others only properties with more than five units or only in specific areas of a city. Before spending your time on anything else, find out if the company will even take on the job.

What experience do you have? Ideally, aim to hire a property manager who has had experience with similar property types for a significant time period—the more years operating, the better. For example, a four-bed, four-bath property could require a different strategy than one with four bachelor apartments. Experience in your local area is also important, since the appropriate rental price to ask, code compliance requirements, and the best places to advertise your vacancies vary from one town to the next.

What certification and training do you have? Regulations for this profession vary widely; some provinces require certification, while others have few or no rules at all. Check to see whether the province you are buying property in has any such certification, and if so, make sure any prospective property manager adheres to the requirements. Look for their designation as a professional property manager, membership in property management associations and/or real estate investment clubs, proper insurance coverage, and continuing education.

How long will it take to receive a response? Can everything be responded to within a few hours or will it take a few business days? Will the tenants receive the same level of responsiveness? What about potential renters? Are there systems in place to deal with urgent maintenance items in a timely manner?

How much will your services cost? Property management companies charge in many ways—be sure you're clear on what the total cost of services will be. Percentage of gross rent, flat fee, or a charge per visit to the property are all common billing practices. Some companies will charge an additional fee for each unit rented; others will charge a higher monthly fee but include this service in the cost. Watch out for companies that charge a premium on any work done on the property in addition to the amount billed out by contractors, or that make use of a maintenance company that is owned by the property management company. These practices have the potential for conflicts of interest.

How much involvement can I have in making decisions about the property? Many property management companies will expect—and some *demand*—that, once they're hired, the property owner (you, the investor) be hands-off in the day-to-day operations of the property. When choosing a company, be clear with your expectations about when you want to be contacted. Confirm they will manage a property where you can maintain a level of control that you are comfortable with. You should authorize necessary maintenance to a certain cost level ($1,000, for example) before you need to be contacted for further approval. This allows for routine maintenance to be performed and for the property owner (you, the investor) to get more involved when capital improvements are needed. The same approach can apply in any situations where the property owner would like to provide input, such as:

- prior to approving a potential renter

- the cost, wording, and placement of advertisements

- potential renter and current resident rental incentive programs

- non-required upgrades (adding a dishwasher, air conditioning, upgrading materials for aesthetic and not maintenance purposes)

CHOOSING YOUR TEAM MEMBERS

An experienced investor-savvy realtor can prove valuable in referring you to professionals who are located in the area you're considering investing in. When I'm working with a new client who is looking, for example, for a lawyer, I usually provide three referrals. It's important to find someone you're comfortable with, and sometimes it's just a matter of matching personality types. I make the introduction, but it's always—*always*—the client's decision who they work with.

TAHANI'S TIP

If any agent tries to influence you—or worse, tells you that you *must* use a specific lawyer, home inspector, or any other professional service—it may be time to find a new realtor. Real estate agents are prohibited by law from pressuring clients into using *any* service. They are free to make referrals and recommendations based on past experiences with previous clients and deals—but who to work with is always the client's decision.

Furthermore, agents must disclose if they are receiving a referral fee or any kind of compensation for recommending someone. This notice must be in writing, and you, the client, must sign off to acknowledge that you've been made aware and approve of such an arrangement.

I, personally, am never compensated for referrals. I recommend lawyers, inspectors, or other professionals for one reason and one reason only: I am happy with how they've dealt with my clients who have used their services. I consider those professionals an extension of my relationship with my clients, so if I recommend someone unworthy, that reflects poorly on me and jeopardizes my relationship with my clients.

TAHANI'S TIP

Always ask your realtor if they receive referral fees from any professional he or she recommends to you. By law, this information must be disclosed to you, in writing, and you must sign off on it.

Bird-Dogging: A Question of Ethics

This raises the prospect of another sometimes-unsavoury practice you may come across in real estate investing—bird-dogging.

Bird-dogging in real estate involves someone who scouts properties on behalf of investors. If the investor buys the recommended property, the bird-dog is paid a "finder's fee," which can range from a few hundred to several thousand dollars.

While technically not illegal in Canada, bird-dogging can lead to some unscrupulous practices, such as the bird-dog learning and divulging private information that may not be in the seller's best interests. For example, let's say a bird-dog learned of a property for sale because the seller, someone he plays hockey with, is going through a divorce. The bird-dog could then discreetly pass this information on to a potential buyer or investor, who then knows the seller might be willing to accept a lower price to facilitate a quick sale. The bird-dog not only betrays the trust of his hockey teammate, he accepts a fee for it, while the buyer acquires a property, possibly at less than market value.

Not all bird-dogging arrangements are as unscrupulous, since they may only involve scouting potential properties and not the release of confidential information or taking advantage of someone's misfortune.

However, there are some very specific restrictions on how any such information may or may not be divulged in real estate transactions, which we address in Chapter 3.

The above discussion underlines the importance of staffing your team with professionals you can trust, who understand your goals and objectives and can help you achieve them.

FEE STRUCTURES FOR YOUR TEAM OF EXPERTS

- **Real estate lawyer:** A lawyer protects your rights and interests as a consumer, and it is imperative to have your lawyer review any offers or agreements. This is especially true with condominium purchases, since these deals are more complex and often involve lengthy contracts. Fees vary depending on the transaction, but generally range from about $750 to $1,200 for each sale or purchase.

- **Lender:** A banker or mortgage broker helps you through the mortgage pre-approval and approval processes, matching you up with financing that best suits your needs and financial situation. Banks are interested in lending you money themselves, while brokers can offer a variety of mortgage products from different types of lenders. Brokers' fees are usually paid by the lender; banks and lenders make their money from interest on the mortgage.

- **Accountant:** An accountant focuses on the tax implications of your personal and rental property finances to make sure you comply with Canada Revenue Agency regulations. He or she can also help you structure your real estate business to minimize taxes paid from the outset and to avoid potentially expensive audits and penalties. Fees for accounting services vary, depending on whether they're oversee-ing your personal taxes as well and on the complexity of your real estate business. Experienced investors stress it's essential to find a good accountant, so it's important to get estimates from three prospective firms and compare their fees and the level of expertise and services offered.

- **Insurance broker:** An insurance broker, much like a mortgage broker, finds the appropriate insurance coverage depending on a buyer's needs and potential discounts. For example, if you own multiple investment properties and you insure them through the same provider, or if you add your own home and car insurance, you can receive significant discounts. Rental properties must be insured as such, and tenants will need their own policies. Fees vary depending on the size, age, and location of the property, but generally range from $500 to $1,000 per year.

- **Property manager:** Property management firms provide a variety of services, generally under two areas: full-service property management and rental agency services. Full-service property management includes maintenance services, rent collection, and financial administration. Acting as a rental agency, a property manager can also assist investor-landlords with marketing their properties, preparing leases and the rental units themselves, coordinating viewings, and screening tenants. The costs for the services vary, depending on the type and size of prop-erty and the number of rental units, but they're generally calculated on a percentage of gross rent, flat fee, or charge-per-visit basis.

GUEST COMMENTARY

An investor-savvy agent is a critical member of your team—but you are still the boss

By Thomas Beyer, Prestigious Properties Canada Ltd., Vancouver, B.C.

An investor-savvy agent is a critical part of your team because, being an investor themselves, they understand your goals and strategy and can assist you with due diligence, finding properties, financing, and property analysis. Their role is essential, but you're still the boss. Think of it as being the chief executive officer of your own company.

Some realtors will push properties on a prospective buyer, regardless of whether the properties fit his or her objectives. They want to make the sale, receive a commission, and get out, and an investor may then be stuck with a property that doesn't suit their plan.

The key advice for novice investors is to go slowly—don't be too trusting, since many sellers exaggerate their numbers and some realtors paint an unrealistically rosy picture.

Your job as the investor is to verify all the numbers with records (such as actual utility bills, tax receipts, rent records, and insurance payments) *for yourself*. Don't assume the vendor or their agent is being completely accurate and honest; it's not that they are necessarily being dishonest, but you have to do the math and prove the numbers yourself as part of your due diligence.

Find a mentor, build your team (realtor, property manager, accountant, lawyer, appraiser, engineer, and even spouse), and educate yourself before doing any deals. *Then* you can write offers—not the other way around.

One mistake could be a very expensive graduation from the real estate investing school of hard knocks.

6 Real Estate Investment Strategies

Starting out as a real estate investor can seem like a daunting process. Where to invest? What type of property should I buy? Which strategy is right for me? For many new investors, it is difficult to know where to begin. Here are three key points that will help you choose the right investment strategy to get started, with confidence.

DETERMINE YOUR OBJECTIVES

You need to be clear about what you want to get out of investing in real estate. Are you looking for something short- or long-term? Are you going to focus on cash flow only, or on equity growth as well? To achieve these objectives, how hands-on do you want to be? How much time and effort do you want to dedicate to your real estate business? How much knowledge and experience do you have?

These are important considerations that you should think about well in advance of your first transaction. Once you have a clear idea of what you're looking to get out of (and put into) your investment, you can begin to seek the right strategy.

FILTER YOUR OPTIONS

After doing your research on the various strategies available to you, start filtering your options. Evaluate the pros and cons of each strategy and see how they fit with your investment objectives.

SPEAK WITH EXPERTS

For each of your top strategies, find someone who is an expert in that strategy. Many veteran real estate investors are happy to share their knowledge with new investors, and hearing about their experiences will give you insight into whether the strategy they used will be a good fit for you.

Time spent doing this kind of homework will pay off in the end. Learning from other investors who have taken the same steps you're about to take could save you—or earn you—thousands of dollars. Being prepared will instill confidence as you figure out which areas, strategies, and properties might be best for you.

COMMON REASONS INVESTORS FAIL

1. **Lack of focus and a business plan:** Many investors try every strategy possible, with a fraction of the focus they need to succeed. Pick one strategy, document it in a business plan, and master it before considering moving on to a second strategy.

2. **Lack of a strong mentor or support network:** It is always a good idea to get advice from a mentor and other experts—people who have "been there and done that." They will point out unnecessary risks, offer solutions, and even help you salvage deals or situations that you think are doomed to failure.

3. **Wrong strategy:** Many investors are followers who do what everyone else is doing, or they choose a strategy that does not work in their market. Some of the most successful investors make a point of doing exactly what everyone else is not doing. Do your homework and choose the right strategy for you, your objectives, and your market.

4. **Lack of effort and time:** This may seem obvious, but many new investors get excited and work hard for a short period in the beginning, then they back off and do nothing. You have to write down your goals and what it will take to achieve them, put together daily tasks, and complete those tasks on a consistent basis.

5. **Lack of knowledge:** I have seen my share of messy deals—from do-it-yourselfers who do everything poorly to inexperienced investors who get in way over their heads. Make sure you fully understand your strategy and have the knowledge, the systems, and the team in place to succeed. And always be thorough in your due diligence.

Acquiring and operating an investment property is very different from buying your primary residence. You're in business, and your number one goal, clearly, is to generate profit. There are various ways to do that, with the most common investment strategies being:

- buy and hold

- fix and flip

- buy, reno, and hold

BUY AND HOLD

This strategy involves buying a property with the intention of keeping it and renting it out over the long term, say a minimum of five to seven years, with the goal of generating positive cash flow. Positive cash flow means renting out the property for more than your monthly mortgage payment and other costs, such as condo fees, taxes, insurance, property management fees, general maintenance, and advertising—all of which you, as owner-landlord, are responsible for.

This strategy is a conservative yet effective way of starting out in real estate investing. It is simple to understand and not overwhelming to execute, since it is basic business: income − expenses = profit.

The benefits of generating positive cash flow are threefold: 1) you pocket the monthly surplus, called positive cash flow; 2) you build equity over the long term while your tenant pays your mortgage, called mortgage paydown; and 3) eventually, when you sell the property after five to seven years or more, you benefit from the appreciation in its value—you sell it for more than what you paid.

With the federal government's mortgage rule changes, which took effect in April 2010, buyers are now required to make a minimum 20-per-cent down payment for investment properties. This larger down payment means that you have to borrow less and your monthly payments will be lower, and the cash flow will be higher.

For example, if you buy a $200,000 investment property, and put down 20 per cent, or $40,000, your mortgage would be $160,000. At an interest rate of 4.5 per cent with a 30-year amortization, your monthly payment would be $810.69. To generate positive cash flow, you would have to be able to successfully charge rent in excess of that amount plus your other operating expenses.

To run the numbers on a prospective property, for a Mortgage Calculator or Affordability Calculator, visit www.realestateriches book.com. All you have to do is plug in your numbers, including the mortgage amount, term, and interest rate, to see what your monthly payment would be. With this tool, you will be able to easily see how any prospective property measures up, helping you to make your purchasing decision.

GUEST COMMENTARY

Buy and hold: The best strategy for novice real estate investors

By Neil Uttamsingh, FirstRentalProperty.com, Toronto, Ont.

Novice real estate investors often struggle at the beginning of their careers, and one of the biggest challenges they face is choosing which investment strategy to use. My personal favourite, and the only one I have used for years, is buy, hold, and rent. I like this strategy for two reasons:

Mortgage paydown

With this strategy, someone else—your tenant—pays down your mortgage on the property, and you watch as your mortgage balance decreases year after year. When I receive the mortgage statements for the properties I own, the first thing I look at is the current mortgage balance. I compare the figure to the balance from the previous year to see how much the mortgage was paid down—again, by someone other than me. It's an excellent reminder of why this strategy works.

Cash flow

Another benefit to the buy and hold strategy is the cash flow that the property generates. Generally speaking, experienced real estate investors purchase properties that produce a positive monthly cash flow—meaning that the total amount of rent they collect is higher than their total monthly expenses.

If you are a novice real estate investor, the most important goal when purchasing properties using this strategy is to make sure they are cash-flow positive on a monthly basis. You will need to put aside this surplus in anticipation of completing future repairs and renovations on your properties.

The powerful factor that begins to take shape as you hold a property for years is that the cash flow generally increases. This happens because your tenants have been paying down your mortgage, as the monthly payments reduce the balance owing. If you continue to rent your property at market rates and you take the opportunity to increase your rents when appropriate, you will benefit from increased monthly cash flow. Cash flow can also increase when your mortgage term is up and you renegotiate. After a five-year term, your mortgage principal balance is reduced because you have been paying it down, so when you renew, your payments will be lower. As long as you charge the same rent, or more, your cash flow will increase.

The importance of working with an investor-savvy realtor

I began investing in real estate in May 2005, when I bought my first rental property. Over the years, I have spoken to other experienced investors, and it has become obvious to me that most new investors don't realize the importance of an investment strategy. Most investors who end up purchasing multiple properties have a clearly defined strategy. So, before you buy your first property, determine your overall investment strategy. It will be a great help to you.

However, figuring out your investment strategy is easier said than done, and it is often the first stumbling block for new investors. They deliberate too much over this point, important though it is, because they don't have the experience to select the best cash-flowing properties or those that will have the greatest potential for appreciation.

This is where an investor-savvy realtor can help. Indeed, an experienced realtor who has knowledge of investment real estate is a critical member of your team. Investor-savvy realtors have a great insight into the local area in which they work—such as what types of properties are selling, the sales trends, who is buying, and what you, as an investor, will be able to rent the properties for. It is essential that you find and use an investor-savvy agent as your guide.

In my case, finding the right realtor who understood real estate investing was one of the smartest things I have done. Using the realtor's local market expertise, I found properties that increased in value over the time I owned them, rented well to quality tenants who paid down my mortgages, and generated positive cash flow. These three benefits are what buy, hold, and rent is all about, and why it's the best strategy for novice real estate investors.

CASE STUDY: BUY AND HOLD STRATEGY PAYS OFF FOR LUISA

Let's talk about Luisa, an investor in her early 30s who, on her own, bought two investment properties in Toronto. She had long been interested in real estate investing; she did her own extensive research, closely following the news on the housing market, and was always on the lookout for new listings in her area.

Luisa purchased those first two properties in Toronto using this method—virtually on her own, with no help or expertise from an investment group or an experienced agent. She would constantly view new listings and call the listing agents of properties she was interested in for more information. She would ask lots of questions and work the numbers herself to calculate how much rent she would have to charge for a prospective property in order to cover the mortgage payment and other monthly costs.

Now, what Luisa did right, of course, was take the time to do thorough research, never making quick, emotional decisions, and always doing all the due diligence necessary to make sure any target property would generate positive cash flow. You would be surprised how many investors don't take these necessary and important steps, even *with* the help of a realtor or investment group, so Luisa deserves full marks for her initiative.

What Luisa didn't do, however, was follow a strategy—because she didn't have one. She understood the basic plan was to buy a property, hold on to it for a long period, and rent it out—key characteristics of what essentially is the buy and hold strategy. But she did not choose the area for its strong economic fundamentals, nor did she know where the local market was in terms of the real estate cycle.

Basically, on her own, Luisa got lucky.

Luisa then found me via the Internet, when she was interested in investing in my area, Kitchener-Waterloo and Cambridge (KWC). When we met and I explained all the growth and development in the area, and what it all meant in terms of real estate opportunities, her jaw dropped. "How can a realtor give me that much information and know so much about investing?" she asked.

We agreed to work together, and in the first year, she bought three properties. Let's talk about the first one: a semi-detached house purchased for $174,000. It didn't need much work, other than some paint and basic freshening up.

Luisa put down the required 20 per cent, about $34,800, and mortgaged the balance of $139,200. She was cash-flowing more than $140 per month.

Fast-forward four years or so, and the cash flow is almost $300 per month: she increased her rent by $150 per month since she bought the property.

Her tenant is paying down her mortgage, while her cash flow also increases. In addition, the value of the property has grown from $174,000 to $214,000. That's $40,000—more than the entire amount of her down payment.

Luisa's Property Analysis (purchase price: $174,000; reno costs: $5,000; total investment: $179,000)

Purchase Price			$174,000
Financing Information			**Amount**
1st Mortgage	80%		$139,200
2nd Mortgage	0%		$0
Investment			**Amount**
Down Payment			$34,800
Land Transfer Tax			$1,465
Immediate Repairs and Renovations			$5,000
Inspection			$371
Appraisal			$239
Title Insurance			$266
Financing Costs			$0
Legal Costs (including disbursements)			$1,600
Staying Power Fund (2 months' rent)			$2,600
Other			$0
Total Investment			$46,341

Income		Monthly	Annually
Gross Rents		$1,300.00	$15,600
Laundry		$0.00	$0
Other Rents		$0.00	$360
Total Income		$1,300.00	$15,960

Operating Expenses	%	Monthly	Annually
Heating		$0.00	$0
Electricity		$0.00	$0
Water / Sewer		$0.00	$0
Property Taxes		$166.67	$2,000
Condo Fees (if applicable)		$0.00	$0
Insurance		$50.00	$600
Property Management	5.0%	$65.00	$780
Rental Pool Management	0.0%	$0.00	$0
Repairs and Maintenance	5.0%	$65.00	$780
Resident Manager		$0.00	$0

Snow Removal				$0.00	$0
Lawn Maintenance				$0.00	$0
Pest Control				$0.00	$0
Other (e.g., rented equipment: hot water heater)				$0.00	$0
Total Operating Expenses				$346.67	$4,160

Operating Income			%	**Monthly**	**Annually**
Operating Income				$953.33	$11,800
Less: Vacancy Allowance			5.0%	$65.00	$780
Net Operating Income (NOI)				$888.33	$11,020

Financing Costs	**Type**	**Amort**	**Rate**	**Monthly**	**Annually**
1st Mortgage Payment	P + I	35	3.79%	$596.50	$7,158
2nd Mortgage Payment	Int Only	25	0.00%	$0.00	$0
Total Financing Payments				$596.50	$7,158

Cash Flow				**Monthly**	**Annually**
Cash Flow Before Taxes				$291.83	$3,862
CAP Rate (ROA)					6.33%
Debt Coverage Ratio (DCR) – Your View					1.54
Debt Coverage Ratio (DCR) – Lender's View					1.46

Return on Investment			**Rate**	**Amount**	**Return**
Cash Return				$3,862.01	8.33%
Mortgage Paydown				$1,956.99	4.22%
Appreciation			3.0%	$5,220.00	11.26%
Total Return on Investment (ROI)					23.82%

This is a powerful example because it shows just how well you can do as an investor in a short period. The three properties Luisa owns in the KWC area are doing well, and she recently called me saying she was ready to buy more, which she did.

The strategy and the process we used to select the properties were similar to the ones I use with all new clients. Other than hearing that the KWC area was a strong prospective market, Luisa didn't really have any knowledge as to *why* it was strong, specifically where it was strong, or which properties to buy based on the local fundamentals.

When I meet with clients, I start by explaining the area and what investors should look for, depending on which strategy they want to use. I give a broad idea of the options, and we then dig deeper to examine each one.

Let's look at an example of how this works. I often show clients a map of the city, and we discuss the various areas and what characterizes each: one neighbourhood may have mostly condos or townhomes, another might have mostly semis or single-detached homes. We discuss the tenant profile each area attracts, the purchase prices of prospective properties, rental rates, and cash flow potential, and we weigh and compare the advantages and disadvantages of each scenario.

We dissect the areas so the investor has a very clear idea of each and understands what strategy would work best there. Clients typically leave this initial meeting satisfied that they understand the area and its potential, as well as the various options open to them.

The key areas to explore for each prospective neighbourhood and property are:

- price range for target properties

- property type and which is the best value and has the higher potential return on investment

- vacancy rate and rental rate

- appreciation potential for the property based on growth and development in the area

- how much work each property requires to make it desirable for renters

- exit strategy: how easy will it be to sell later on, and with what strategy

Even if a property's value rises by an average of only 3 per cent per year (a relatively conservative amount), the $200,000 property you buy today will be worth approximately $242,000 in seven years. Remember, appreciation plus mortgage paydown plus cash flow equals profits. Multiply that by however many properties you may eventually own and you'll see why the buy and hold strategy makes so much sense over the long term. In my opinion, buy and hold is the best and most suitable strategy for novice investors.

FIX AND FLIP

Often seen on real estate TV shows, the fix and flip involves buying a property that needs work. The condition of the property likely means it's undervalued, and the investors plan to renovate it over a period of weeks or months and then "flip" it in short order for a profit. This method can yield high returns, but also carries high risks because of the capital costs required for renovations and the possibility that you may need to hold on to the property longer than anticipated if you can't sell it quickly.

This strategy is more suited to experienced investors, but even they need to be careful. Not only do they need a lot of money up front but also delays can be very costly. For example, if a contractor hired for the job doesn't complete it on schedule, or more time is required than originally planned, or permits are delayed, the investor is on the hook for extra costs, and possibly additional mortgage and interest payments—which means less profit.

CASE STUDY: WHEN A FIX AND FLIP BECOMES A FIX AND *FLOP*

Here's an excellent example of how easily a fix and flip can go off the rails, and how dangerous and costly it can be—quickly becoming a fix and flop.

This is a true story from 2009, involving a detached home in Toronto, measuring about 2,500 square feet, with a two-car garage and a decent-sized lot in an established area. Built in the 1970s, the home's original owners, an elderly couple, sold it in order to downsize to smaller quarters in a retirement community. They sold it for about $450,000, an average and fair price for the area and the home type.

A young couple in their 30s bought the place, with plans to reno-vate to modernize the outdated feel and decor and to flip the property for what they hoped were quick, large profits. They spent about four months on the renovations, installing a new kitchen island, all-new stainless steel appliances, new flooring throughout to replace old carpeting, and new doors and trims and light fixtures. They also fin-ished the large basement, sectioning off the cold cellar and other separate rooms. Total spent for the project? A whopping $215,000. Yes, *$215,000*.

Once the project was complete and ready to "flip," the couple listed the property—advertising "ultra-modern features and com-pletely renovated top to bottom," for $736,000.

The property sat on the market for six months; after changing realtors twice and discounting the asking price twice, the own-ers finally took the property off the market. Unable to sell it, they moved in themselves and leased out the basement as a second-ary suite.

How did this flip become a flop?

1. Unsophisticated investors

2. No real plan

3. No real knowledge of real estate investing

4. Unrealistic expectations

5. Refusal to listen to realtor advice

The appropriate amount to spend on a fix and flip varies depend-ing on the condition of the property, local market fundamentals, and other factors. However, any investor who has ever succeeded with this strategy will stress that one of the key determining factors is where the house is, vis-à-vis neighbourhood averages and compa-rables. You can't spend an unlimited amount without regard for what's around you. In other words, you can't drop a mansion in the middle of a downtrodden area and expect it to fetch the same price it would if it was in an area of other luxury homes. Location matters, and in this case, as beautifully as the renovated home showed, the surrounding properties were showing their age, and the neighbourhood in general looked to be on the decline.

Worse, one of the properties immediately adjacent—quite literally one of the first things you would see when you stepped out the front door of this property—was a neglected house in serious disrepair, with broken windows, unkempt yard, and other eyesores.

This couple, whether inspired by greed or naivety, spent a totally unrealistic amount (47 per cent of the purchase price) on renovations, based on what they should have realistically hoped to sell the house for in this particular area. Other similarly modernized properties in the area were selling for $550,000 to $575,000. There was no way in the world the owners would recoup their $215,000 reno costs, let alone turn a profit.

These "investors" will be paying dearly for this fix and flop for a long time, and may be hard pressed to ever recoup their investment.

BUY, RENO, AND HOLD

There is a third option, a makeshift strategy called buy, reno, and hold, which is a combination of buy and hold and fix and flip. Also known as a "long-term flip," this strategy is similar to a fix and flip because it involves buying a property that needs work but is in a desirable area. Perhaps it was neglected or was lived in by long-term owners who didn't keep up with modern decor—imagine a home with lots of 1970s wood panelling, wallpaper, or paint colour.

The typical fix and flip, or short-term flip, is generally more risky because you're counting both on renovations to increase the value in short order and on a quick sale to produce profits. A lot of people get excited about this strategy because TV shows have made it look easy to make a lot of money quickly.

The buy, reno, and hold strategy is generally less risky because it involves *holding* and renting out the property after you've renovated it, so you will benefit from the mortgage paydown and value appreciation, before selling.

If a client insists on doing a flip, I always stress to them that the buy, reno, and hold is a great fallback strategy if their original plan doesn't generate enough profit, or if the market softens and a quick flip isn't possible.

CASE STUDY: FRED DECIDES TO BUY, RENO, AND HOLD

One of my clients, Fred, began investing in real estate about two years before we met. He had already purchased two properties in my area, and three in different areas close to where he lives, which he bought through the listing agents. Just like Luisa, Fred searched for prospective investment properties himself, by viewing listings in the newspaper and on the MLS®. He also used a different realtor for each purchase, as well as a different home inspector and so on. Not only is searching for prospective properties this way very time-consuming for investors but also, by the time listings hit the MLS®, many of the best deals are often gone; savvy realtors can present properties to their clients before they hit the market.

Fred initially contacted me because of a listing I had advertised in the newspaper. We talked for a few minutes, and I answered his questions. I wasn't sure what to make of it. A few weeks later, Fred called back and said he would like to meet with me, since he was impressed with my knowledge and wanted to know more about working with me. A meeting would be good for me as well, since it would help me to better understand Fred's goals, and his level of knowledge and experience in real estate investing.

Fred is an average, hard-working family man with three kids. He wanted to buy more investment properties, but didn't know how. When we met, one of the first things he expressed was his frustration that most realtors lacked the knowledge needed to help investors. In particular, he had been frustrated that his previous agent did not have a team of other professionals to whom he could refer Fred. Any question Fred asked this realtor, the answer was always "I don't know." That type of response is acceptable—if it's followed by "I will find out." But Fred's agent didn't know how—or didn't *want*—to take the extra steps to help his client.

I looked at the two properties he had previously bought in my area. They were generating only average positive cash flow. Fred wanted to invest in properties with higher cash flow and better-than-average value appreciation. He said he wanted to use the buy, reno, and hold strategy, thinking that this would produce his desired returns; but he also said he was scared to death, because he thought it would be time-consuming and could be riskier than his current buy and hold properties.

The two homes Fred bought were okay, but were located in mature areas where there was very little sales activity. There wasn't a lot of growth or development, which meant property appreciation was at the lower end of the scale, as was the tenant profile.

Even though Fred took action and bought the properties on his own, he wasn't exactly thrilled with how they were performing. So, when we met, I explained a few different local areas to him, drilling down into specific neighbourhoods. I walked him through the fundamentals of each area, the growth and economic developments taking place there, the various tenant profiles, which areas were in greater demand and, ultimately, where he could buy investment properties that would generate more rental income and higher appreciation.

Fred was happy—so happy that he brought his whole family to our next meeting.

Knowing that he wanted to use the buy, reno, and hold strategy, we discussed the type of property he wanted: freehold (outright ownership) with no monthly condo fees. We decided on a semi-detached house in an area where there was a lot of development and growth, and where most tenants would be happy to live.

This is a perfect illustration of the benefits of working with an investor-savvy realtor: three weeks after Fred and I met, an out-of-town agent I know called to say that he had a property—a semi-detached house that happened to be in the area Fred and I were looking at— and asked if I knew of someone who might be interested. The timing was perfect. The property hadn't yet been listed, and we would have first crack at it.

Fred's Property Analysis (purchase price: $198,000; reno costs: $8,900; total investment: $206,900)

Purchase Price		$198,000
Financing Information		**Amount**
1st Mortgage	80%	$158,400
2nd Mortgage	0%	$0
Investment		**Amount**
Down Payment		$39,600
Land Transfer Tax		$1,705
Immediate Repairs and Renovations		$8,900
Inspection		$371
Appraisal		$239
Title Insurance		$266
Financing Costs		$0
Legal Costs (including disbursements)		$1,600
Staying Power Fund (2 months' rent)		$2,800
Other		$0
Total Investment		$55,481

Income		Monthly	Annually
Gross Rents		$1,350.00	$16,200
Laundry		$0.00	$0
Other Rents		$0.00	$360
Total Income		$1,350.00	$16,560

Operating Expenses	%	Monthly	Annually
Heating		$0.00	$0
Electricity		$0.00	$0
Water / Sewer		$0.00	$0
Property Taxes		$200.00	$2,400
Condo Fees (if applicable)		$0.00	$0
Insurance		$50.00	$600
Property Management	7.0%	$94.50	$1,134
Rental Pool Management	0.0%	$0.00	$0
Repairs and Maintenance	5.0%	$67.50	$810
Resident Manager		$0.00	$0
Snow Removal		$0.00	$0

				$0.00	$0
Lawn Maintenance				$0.00	$0
Pest Control				$0.00	$0
Other (e.g., rented equipment: hot water heater)				$0.00	$0
Total Operating Expenses				$412.00	$4,944

Operating Income		%		Monthly	Annually
Operating Income				$938.00	$11,616
Less: Vacancy Allowance		5.0%		$67.50	$810
Net Operating Income (NOI)				$870.50	$10,806

Financing Costs	Type	Amort	Rate	Monthly	Annually
1st Mortgage Payment	P + I	35	3.79%	$678.77	$8,145
2nd Mortgage Payment	Int Only	25	0.00%	$0.00	$0
Total Financing Payments				$678.77	$8,145

Cash Flow				Monthly	Annually
Cash Flow Before Taxes				$191.73	$2,661
CAP Rate (ROA)					5.46%
Debt Coverage Ratio (DCR) – Your View					1.33
Debt Coverage Ratio (DCR) – Lender's View					1.30

Return on Investment			Rate	Amount	Return
Cash Return				$2,660.70	4.80%
Mortgage Paydown				$2,226.92	4.01%
Appreciation			3.0%	$5,940.00	10.71%
Total Return on Investment (ROI)					19.52%

I called Fred with the news, and he came over as soon as he could, knowing that if we didn't take action immediately, we might soon have competition. I sent Fred the comparables for the recently sold semis in the area—and they were mostly around $220,000 to $225,000. I also e-mailed him details for two other homes that were for sale at $224,900. I estimated that our target property would rent for about $1,395, with tenants paying heat, hydro, and water.

The agent was going to list the house at $214,900; we offered $198,000—and it was accepted. Because the house was a power of sale (when the bank takes over the house due to mortgage default), it needed some work. As little as $4,000 in improvements would have brought it up to market standard, but Fred wanted to do more so he could charge above-average rent.

He ended up installing new laminate flooring on the main and upper floors, and painting the entire interior. He also changed the countertop in the kitchen and all the light fixtures in the house, plus he did some minor landscaping. In total, Fred spent $8,700.

So now his costs were $198,000 plus $8,700, for a total investment of $206,700. Once the enhancements were made, he refinanced the property and had an appraisal done, which came in at $224,000. This meant he got back his reno investment right away—and then some: $224,000 (the new appraised value) minus $206,700 (his total investment) equals $17,300 (the return in value appreciation). In addition, the house in that market would have listed at $229,900 and likely have sold for that since it showed extremely well with all the updates.

Not only did Fred benefit from our relationship—the guidance I provided him, as well as the early notice that this property was coming up for sale—but he also gained access to the expertise he was looking for through the team members I recommended. He ended up renting the property for $1,350 to a family who had been renting one of his other houses in the area—who were willing to pay $200 more than their existing rent to be in a nicer home in a better neighbourhood.

Note: I usually advise my investor-clients to budget about 5 to 10 per cent of the purchase price for the renovation. The fact that Fred brought the house's value up by 13 per cent while investing only about 4.5 per cent of the purchase price meant he was already doing well.

By choosing to buy, reno, and hold, Fred was in a very strong position. He now had a great property that was among the best in the neighbourhood and was sure to appreciate in value over five to seven years. While renting it out, he was able to charge more than the average rent, and because the property had strong appeal, there would be more competition for it among good tenants.

Doing a straight flip is more risky. I have heard many sad stories of people losing lots of money because they think it's easy. They don't realize the setbacks—contractors who don't show up, costs that skyrocket over budget, permit delays and costs, and other headaches that can quickly erode profit potential—to say nothing of the potential for market conditions to soften by the time the reno is complete and the property is ready to sell.

For experienced investors who may have joint venture partners who are handymen or experienced in home renovations, maybe a quick flip makes some sense. But if you are my client, a new or novice investor, and you come to me with such a plan mostly because you saw it on TV? We're going to have a serious conversation—and I would suggest a buy, reno, and hold instead.

AVOIDING TEMPTATION

Once you have acquired a few investment properties using the buy and hold strategy, you may be tempted to consider other investment methods that require a little more experience and knowledge—and that also may carry more risk. Of course, there is no blanket piece of advice for this scenario, since everyone will have different risk tolerances. You may come across an opportunity that on the surface is too good to pass up (always do your due diligence) or that may involve a joint venture partner or that has other features that make the deal worth considering. Generally speaking, though, it's safer to stick with the same plan that got you to where you are: buy and hold. But if you're itching to be a little more aggressive with your strategy, consider:

- a fix and flip—it will take more knowledge and more capital investment and is a bit riskier than buying, holding, and renting, but the return can be higher

- a rezoning scenario—perhaps a property you're interested in buying has vacant land beside it, and you might be able to purchase that lot as well and redevelop both, but this takes time

- an addition—you could undertake a renovation to add an extra unit to one of your existing rental properties

I mention these alternative strategies as examples of ventures you might consider once you gain some experience as an investor. Certainly there are plenty of investors I know who began with simple purchases and who, before too long, expanded into other, more ambitious approaches. However, the common denominator throughout any of these strategies should always be the fundamentals.

PART II

INVESTMENT STRATEGIES AND DUE DILIGENCE

7 Financing Strategies

When it comes to buying an investment property, most people don't have enough cash to buy it outright, so they take out a mortgage. This is considered a form of leverage because you use your pool of capital to access more capital, with the hope that you will generate higher returns.

Leverage can be a powerful tool. For example, when you buy a guaranteed investment certificate or a bond for $50,000, only that $50,000 is working for you—making you money at whatever the current interest rate is. If instead you use that $50,000 as a down payment to buy a $200,000 property, taking out a mortgage for the remaining 75 per cent, you make money on the entire $200,000, not just on the 25 per cent you contributed.

If that $200,000 property appreciates an average of 3 per cent each year for five years, your gain is: $200,000 × 3% = $6,000 × 5 years = $30,000. That's a 60-per-cent appreciation on your original investment of $50,000 in five years! What other investment vehicle offers you such returns? Plus, add the mortgage paydown and the positive cash flow that investment properties offer, and you can see the real power of leverage in real estate.

Once you have owned your first property for a period of time and it appreciates in value, you can leverage that value by taking out some of the equity and using it to buy other property.

FINANCING FOR INVESTORS

One of the key differences between financing for real estate investing and financing the purchase of your primary residence is how the situation is viewed and handled *by the lender*.

GUEST COMMENTARY

Portfolio lending versus transactional lending

By Peter Kinch, president, Peter Kinch Mortgage Team, Dominion Lending Centres, Vancouver, B.C.

A goal-oriented approach

For years, the majority of bankers and brokers in Canada have been trained to look at each mortgage request that crosses their desk as a *transaction*. That is because the majority of mortgages processed in Canada are for homeowners. As real estate becomes the investment vehicle of choice for more Canadians, a "transactional approach" to their financing could be costly. Real estate investors know they will need to make multiple purchases in order to accomplish their goals. What they don't know is that they need to make those purchases with the understanding that each move now impacts the whole portfolio. They don't have the luxury of taking a transactional approach to their mortgages. Instead, they need to be working with a broker or lender who understands how to take a "portfolio approach."

The difference between a transactional approach and a portfolio approach is like the difference between playing a game of chess at eye level and looking at the board from above. At eye level, you can make a move, but you have no idea how your move may impact the other pieces on the board. If, however, you take a bird's-eye view, you will be able to anticipate the cause and effect of your move before you make it—thus avoiding mistakes. The majority of brokers and bankers have been trained to do a simple (eye-level) task—get you a mortgage. When you come to them and say that you have just pur-chased a property and need a mortgage, if they merely respond to your request, they are focusing on the transaction—not your portfolio.

A broker or banker who understands the portfolio approach will first and foremost ask you about your five-year plan. Taking a simple transactional approach to the mortgage could inadvertently handcuff you from getting future mortgages. They should ask, "What are your goals? What is your plan?" And after asking these questions many times over, I discovered that real estate investors have unique issues that homeowners don't. I also realized that they really have only two major obstacles. One is qualifying for multiple mortgages at the bank, and the second is being able to come up with enough money for down payments on all of their potential purchases. These two obstacles have a cause and effect impact on each other. What you do on one side of the ledger impacts and affects the other. Therefore, it is imperative that you take the portfolio approach to ensure that the decisions you make today do not negatively impact what you might want to do tomorrow.

Transactional lending approach

A common mistake, using the transactional approach, is for an investor to talk to a bank or broker about buying one or two properties. The client explains that he or she has a limited down payment, and instead of putting all the money on one property would rather use high-ratio mortgages to spread the down payment over two. The bank calculates that the investor has enough verifiable income to qualify for the high-ratio mortgages and funds the two deals. Six months later, the same client comes back with two more purchases and a joint venture partner to provide the down payment, but the bank declines the application because the investor's debt-service ratios were maxed out on the previous purchases. The banker then explains that, in spite of the fact that the investor "qualified" for high-ratio mortgages on the first two purchases, the properties now have negative cash flow, so the third purchase puts them over their debt-service limits with the bank. In other words, not asking about the client's goals resulted in poor advice.

Portfolio lending approach

The same client sits down with a broker who understands the portfolio approach and has a pre-positioning consultation. In that meeting, the broker learns that the client has a goal to buy 20 single-family homes or townhouses over the next five years. The broker would then immediately know by looking at their financial statements that it is unlikely the client has enough cash to purchase all of those properties on their own, so they discuss the use of joint venture partners. The broker also knows that the client will likely have to utilize multiple lenders to accomplish this goal, since most lenders have a limit as to how much exposure they want with one client. In addition, the broker will realize that, based on the client's current income, in order to qualify for that many properties, each purchase will need to generate a positive cash flow. This will allow the broker to use the surplus income to help qualify for future deals. As such, the next purchase would need to be made conventionally, with at least 20 per cent down. Not only will this avoid the cost of high-ratio insurance, but it will also aid in creating positive cash flow for the client. Since the client already knew that they would eventually need to attract joint venture capital, the first purchase is structured with this in mind. The surplus from the positive cash flow allows them to qualify for the next purchase, and the portfolio looks more attractive to future joint venture partners.

As a further step, the broker using the portfolio approach will recommend that the client structure both the mortgage on their principal residence and the one on the rental property with a "re-advanceable" mortgage/line of credit combination. This product, which is offered by various lenders in various forms, allows equity created by paying down the mortgage to be re-advanced in the form of a line of credit (LOC). The amount of accessible equity in the LOC will build up every year until there is enough for a future down payment. And, of course, when the money for the down payment comes from the LOC on the principal residence, the interest on the LOC is tax deductible.

When you start with the end result in mind and look at your portfolio from a big-picture perspective, the obstacles become obvious. By simply taking the portfolio approach to arranging your mortgages, you can identify any obstacles well in advance and structure the portfolio to address them before they arise. Understanding the cause and effect that your decision-making process has on the development of your portfolio is the difference between accomplishing your goals and hitting the proverbial brick wall.

GUEST COMMENTARY

Understanding mortgage financing for real estate investors

By Kevin Boughen, Dominion Lending Centres, Toronto, Ont.

Successful investors understand the importance of having a knowledgeable mortgage broker on their team. A broker with a detailed understanding of investment financing will work with the investor to ensure their personal finances, rental property performance, and lender selection are all positioned to help them reach their purchase goals.

For an investor to successfully plan their financing strategy, it is important that they understand how lenders are going to evaluate their applications not only now but also *in the future*. Once an investor owns two or three properties, they are going to be evaluated in a very different way than someone buying their personal home, a vacation property, or their first couple of rental properties. If an investor is not careful with how they structure their financing with every single purchase, they may find that previous financing decisions have brought their financing approvals to an early halt.

Once an investor owns two or three investment properties, lenders effectively divide the investor's finances into two distinct evaluations: their personal finances and the performance of their rental properties. Both must meet minimum financial requirements in order for the investor to continue to receive financing approvals.

Personal finances

Lenders want to make sure that the investors are living within their means. Generally speaking, lenders like to see no more than 40 per cent of the investor's gross monthly income being spent on monthly carrying costs for personal debt.

The most common mistakes investors make when calculating personal gross monthly income

- Investors view existing rental income as personal income. Rent will be used in the rental property evaluation process and will not be counted as part of personal gross monthly income.

- They do not realize that they must have finished any probationary period before their salary income will be considered.

- They do not have a two-year tax history before including bonus, commission, or part-time income.

- They do not have a two-year tax history before including self-employed business income.

Some lenders do offer special financing terms to assist self-employed investors when their self-employed income does not meet traditional guidelines. Larger down payments are typically required in these situations.

The most common mistakes investors make when calculating personal debt

- Investors underestimate the impact of co-signing. When an investor has co-signed for someone else's mortgage, car loan, student loan, or any other debt obligation, the full carrying costs of these obligations are counted as the investor's personal debt, regardless of who is actually making the monthly payments.

- They incorrectly calculate credit card and unsecured line of credit payments. Even though an investor may be utilizing a credit card or unsecured line of credit with a special low monthly payment, the lender will use 3 per cent of the balance as the monthly payment for personal debt calculations.

- They fail to include home equity line of credit (HELOC) products registered against the investor's personal residence or vacation home. Even though these funds may have been used to purchase rental properties, and even though the monthly carrying cost of this debt may be covered by income generated by the rental properties, when the debt is registered against a personal residence the carrying costs are counted against the investor's personal debt.

Performance of the rental properties

By the time an investor is purchasing their third rental property, the lenders start taking a close look at the performance of the existing rental portfolio. Although each lender uses slightly different calculations to evaluate the portfolio, they all want the property's rent to more than cover all the associated operating expenses, including the mortgage payment, property taxes, utilities, and insurance, as well as an allocation for vacancy, maintenance, repairs, and management. This evaluation is sometimes called a Debt Coverage Ratio (DCR) and the minimum target for each property is a DCR of 1.1 or greater.

When an investor has a strong income-to-debt ratio, the profitability of the rental properties being purchased sometimes goes unchecked by the lenders for the first two rental purchases. Profitability is often overlooked when an investor's personal income adequately covers both their personal debt and the carrying costs of the rental properties. This is the most common problem we see among investors who seek financing when they already own one or two properties. They have successfully obtained the wrong type of financing on their previous purchases, and now that they are attempting to buy their third rental property, the lender starts checking the performance of their existing properties and finds the investments do not meet the minimum cash-flow targets to enable the investor to proceed with additional purchases.

The most common mistakes investors make with respect to existing rental financing and DCR calculations

- Investors purchase properties that do not meet minimum cash-flow requirements. The purchase price and/or operating costs are simply too high compared to the rent the property can generate. When this occurs, the investor's ability to purchase additional properties is significantly impacted.

- They choose the wrong amortization period. When purchasing a home to live in, homebuyers are often encouraged to choose the lowest amortization with the highest possible monthly payment they can comfortably afford. This can be a good strategy, as it can save them thousands of dollars in interest and allow them to pay off their mortgage years earlier than with longer amortizations. However, for investors buying rental properties, this is the wrong approach and could bring future purchase plans to an abrupt stop. When it comes to rental financing, it is important to be sure that the amortization and monthly payment facilitate a DCR that will allow you to meet your purchase objectives.

• They make the wrong down payment. Some investors believe they should always make the smallest possible down payment for every purchase—the theory being this will spread their capital further and allow them to purchase more properties. The problem with this approach is that smaller down payments result in larger mortgages and therefore larger monthly carrying costs. If care is not taken to ensure the resulting mortgage payments facilitate an acceptable DCR, you might create a problem that could have been avoided with a larger down payment.

• They do not consider the carrying costs on second mortgages and HELOCs registered against investment properties. When an investment property has a second mortgage or HELOC registered against it, the carrying costs must be included in the DCR calculation for that property, regardless of what the funds were used for or how the carrying costs are actually being paid.

In addition to keeping both their personal income/debt ratios and rental property DCR in check, the successful investor also uses the right lender at the right time in order to meet their purchasing objectives. Each lender has different criteria, depending on how many properties you own.

Some lenders require investors to have a minimum net worth after a certain number of property purchases, depending on their level of personal income; others require minimum liquid assets based on how many properties are in the investor's portfolio. Some lenders will do business with you only if you own fewer than four properties, while others don't mind if you already have sixteen. Only with a detailed understanding of each lender's criteria can an investor successfully choose the right lender at the right time.

Once an investor has chosen the right product with the right terms from the lender best-suited for a specific purchase, the broker/lender will ask for the following important supporting documentation:

- letters of employment

- pay stubs

- Notice(s) of Assessment (NOA) from Canada Revenue Agency

- complete tax returns

- down payment via cash (if coming from cash or liquidated investments, banking statements must confirm that the full down payment has been in the investor's account for at least three months)

- any HELOC statements for down payment (must be less than 30 days old)

- mortgage statements for all existing properties

- property tax bills for all existing properties

- leases for all existing rental properties

OTHER FINANCING OPTIONS

In addition to simply buying an investment property on your own, there are a couple of other interesting financing options available, including lease-to-own tenants and joint venture partnerships.

Lease- or Rent-to-Own

This strategy involves owning and renting a property to a tenant who wants to buy the property at the end of a pre-determined term, usually between one and three years. Typically, these tenants have damaged credit, lack the down payment to buy their own property, or face other personal circumstances, such as divorce or recent job loss, that make it difficult for them to purchase a house in the conventional way.

Tenants pay a premium on their rent every month, and the surplus goes toward their down payment. For example, if fair market rent is $900 per month and the tenant pays $1,200, the investor-owner puts $300 of the monthly payment toward the tenant's down payment, so after two or three years they have saved up a substantial amount.

A rent-to-own plan is good for the investor because there is a clear, short-term exit strategy and a good tenant who's going to care for the property as if it was their own. It's also good for the tenant (owner-in-training) since it helps them buy a house that may have been unavailable to them through traditional financing.

We're not going to get into this strategy in too much detail, since it is very different from the buy and hold strategy that I primarily advise for novice investors. If you want to learn more about rent-to-own, there is an excellent book on the subject by Mark Loeffler—*Investing in Rent-to-Own Property: A Complete Guide for Canadian Real Estate Investors*—also published by John Wiley & Sons Canada, Ltd.

Joint Venture Partnerships

Vendor Take-Back Mortgage: Estimated Cash Flow Analysis

PURCHASE PRICE		$170,000.00	
Financial Breakdown		**Amount**	
Price		$170,000.00	
Down Payment	15%	$25,500.00	
1st Mortgage	75%	$127,500.00	
(new financing, variable rate, 30-yr amort.)			
2nd Mortgage	10%	$170,000.00	
(10% interest only, annual payments)			
	100%		
Income		**Monthly**	**Annually**
Market Rent		$1,300.00	
Vacancy Factor	5%	-$65.00	
Total Income (1st year)		$1,235.00	$14,820.00

Expenses		Monthly	Annually
Property Taxes		-$95.00	
Condo Fees		-$192.00	
Repairs and Maintenance Factor	5%	-$65.00	
Property Management (% of actual rent)	10%	-$123.50	
Insurance		-$20.00	
Total Expenses		-$495.50	-$5,946.00
Cash Flow Before Debt Payment		$739.50	$8,874.00
1st Mortgage Payment *		-$558.27	-$6,699.24
(3.95% interest 1 principle) – 35-yr amort.			
2nd Mortgage Payment		-$141.67	-$1,700.04
(10%, interest only, annual payments)			
Estimated Cash Flow		$39.56	$474.72

* Actual mortgage rate is prime minus 0.6 ($431.61). Monthly payment is set at 5-year fixed rate of 3.95% to maximize mortgage principal reduction.

Joint venture partnership can be a good way for investors to team up and share complementary strengths. For example, one partner might have money to invest while the other has expert knowledge in a specific area or project. The arrangement can be split any way the partners see fit—50/50, 60/40, or whatever suits them. Remember that this, too, is a relationship, so it is imperative that each partner does his or her own due diligence, not just on the investment opportunity but also on the others involved.

Vendor Take-Back Mortgages

A vendor take-back mortgage occurs when the vendor or seller of a property is willing to provide some or all of the mortgage financing on the sale, as opposed to a bank or other financial institution. This typically happens in commercial deals where a purchaser may have difficulty obtaining financing through traditional means. The buyer takes a mortgage out with the vendor and makes payments directly to that vendor; meanwhile, title is transferred to the buyer. Vendor take-back mortgages are often used when the vendor knows and trusts the purchaser.

GUEST COMMENTARY

You can buy real estate without having a lot of money

By Russell Westcott, vice-president, The Real Estate Investment Network; Canadian best-selling co-author, *97 Tips for Canadian Real Estate Investors*

Knowledge will be your capital . . . Integrity your magnet . . . And relationships will be your fuel.

There will come a time when most real estate investors will be looking for secondary sources of cash to build their portfolios. Some will use additional leveraged monies such as lines of credit or equity in the rest of their portfolio or private money. However, one of the most common solutions is bringing a "money partner" into the mix, someone who can provide working capital to fund the portfolio growth and who is looking to get a return on their available cash.

Although this type of relationship is commonly called a joint venture, in many cases it is not technically such. Many times, it could be a shareholder relationship, where the investor and the cash provider own shares of a corporation that they use to invest. In other cases, the money investor just wants a simple, annual percentage return on their investment—this would be a lender relationship.

A true joint venture occurs when two or more parties get together, pool their money and knowledge, and leverage both to build a portfolio. No shares are owned; it is just two or more parties deciding that the best course of action for both is to work together. They agree to terms on money, division of duties, and setting of goals. From that comes a joint venture agreement (or as some people call it, a business prenuptial agreement). This agreement must be detailed and must be completed before any money passes hands, because once real money enters the equation new emotions enter, making the written agreement much more volatile to create. When such an agreement is created, it becomes the basis of the relationship moving forward and deals with all potentialities (taxes, income, expenses, death, divorce, duties, and disputes).

Most of these joint venture deals are structured where one partner finds and negotiates the real estate deal to the absolute best of their ability, while the other partner or partners put up all or part of the cash in return for participating in the ultimate profits in the deal.

They are full partners, each with their own risks in the deal. One is contributing their vast expertise, experience, and contacts to maximize the profits in the deal by choosing the property wisely, arranging a good price, and then managing the day-to-day operations of the property. The other is often a silent partner providing just the initial investment capital. Risks are shared, as are the rewards, mostly on a 50/50 basis (after the money partner is first paid back their capital).

Bringing other people's money into your real estate deals can be a huge win for both parties involved, but I must warn you, it is critical that you look after the other partner's money even better than you would protect your own. In order to make this structure successful and repeatable you must pay extra attention to your due diligence, making sure you're buying into the "right deal." Never put someone else's money into a deal that you wouldn't put your own (or your grandmother's) money into.

Note: Never, ever put someone else's money into a deal that you would not be willing to put your own, your best friend's, or your family's money into.

Never tolerate risks that you, or your investor, wouldn't normally take; explain the risks to the money partner in advance; and keep in close contact with them. If there is bad news, don't hide it. If there is great news, tell them early and often. This is critical, because a successful deal is the best way to attract even more funds to your investment business.

Once you find someone who wants to work with you, the next step is to immediately begin treating it like the business that it is. This is especially important with friends and family, as these relationships are often taken more casually, when they in fact should be taken even more seriously.

GUEST COMMENTARY

Tips to make a joint venture go smoothly

By Todd Millar and Danielle Millar, Glenn Simon Inc., Edmonton, Alta.

To have a joint venture partnership (JVP) operate smoothly and perform effectively, you first need to have the proper balance of partners. Essentially, a JVP is formed to leverage the different strengths of two or more entities for the benefit of reaching a mutual goal. In real estate, JVPs often consist of an expert real estate investor and a money partner who plays the role of the funding investor. There are many shapes and sizes to these partnerships, but a core diligence underlines what you'll need to watch out for before entering into one.

1. Know thy partner: Consider your new JVP as you would a potential spouse. You'll need to ask the real estate expert about the system he or she uses to select a property, the due diligence involved, how funds are allocated or deployed, property management style, track record (has the expert invested in both up and down cycles?), commitment in the deal, and the exit strategy. These are just a few of the primers you need to start the conversation.

If you're working with a potential money partner, you'll ask about investment knowledge, level of risk that he or she is comfortable with, financial ability, expected profit and time frame, and whether he or she is the sole decision maker or if there are other people of influence involved. Do your goals align? Can you both deliver? Remember, these are the starting points to finding out if you are a match; there are still many more questions to ask.

In a long-distance JVP, if you are in the expert role: you are the "person on the ground," so be sure to manage accordingly and keep your partner updated. If you're the money partner: whenever possible, visit the area you're investing in and get a feel for the local demographic. You will need heightened levels of communication to ensure that the joint venture works as smoothly as possible.

2. Good legal documents make good partnerships: There was a time when a man was as good as his word. Nowadays, the complications of life get in the way. Marriages, divorce, bankruptcy, and other unplanned events *will* affect your JVP. Having a clear joint venture agreement template designed will help you navigate the bumps in the road. Both partners should seek their own experienced (JV- and real estate–related) legal advice.

3. Manage expectations: Our mantra has been to "under-promise, over-deliver." You endeavour to do your very best, but at minimum you'll need to fulfill your commitments per the joint venture agreement you signed. In the best JVPs, both partners are willing to see the venture through to the end, trust one another's strengths, and communicate with a solution-oriented attitude that is geared to ultimately serving the good of the JVP.

8

Location, Location, Location

When buying your first couple of properties, consider purchasing in an area within a one- or two-hour drive from where you live, so you can easily visit the property as necessary. But with that said, and while it's important to consider logistics when looking for potential areas to invest in, the main considerations when choosing a location must be the economic fundamentals: above-average job growth, population influx, above-average income growth, increasing yet reasonable property prices, and proximity to mass transit, shopping, schools, and other amenities. Because I tend to focus on the buy and hold strategy with an emphasis on generating positive cash flow over the long term, taking the time to understand the market fundamentals before you buy is particularly important.

FUNDAMENTALS, FUNDAMENTALS, FUNDAMENTALS

So, how do you determine which market is best for you? If you're just starting out in your real estate career, work with an investor-savvy agent who can help you identify areas that are stable and reliable, as opposed to those characterized by a lot of market fluctuations. More seasoned investors might be able to consider a market or property that requires a more risky strategy, but it's not the best plan for beginners. For novice investors, the key determining factor should always be solid local fundamentals.

The economic forces that drive the market are passive factors over which you have no control. The main ones that influence the real estate market are:

Mortgage interest rates

Low interest rates keep expenses down, but also allow renters to become first-time homeowners, leading to increased vacancy rates, so low rates are neutral for investors.

Vacancy and rental market rates

Generally speaking, a vacancy rate of between 2 and 3 per cent is considered a balanced market, so an area with a lower rate than that—and trending down—is a prime potential investment area. A low and declining vacancy rate suggests there is more rental demand than supply, which bodes well for investment properties and the potential to increase rents. Whether the average rent in an area is trending up or down is a direct indicator of rental demand; if rents are rising quickly, that means there's an inadequate supply of rental units, and if they're dropping, that could mean there are too many rental units on the market.

Above-average income growth

If a town's average disposable income is increasing faster than the provincial average, real estate prices are likely to follow. The key indicators of this are increasing average income, decreasing income tax rates, and increasing retail sales.

Job growth and population influx

Areas that are experiencing significant job growth could represent a buying opportunity, because an increase in housing demand without an increase in supply will drive up house prices. It typically takes many months for the housing supply to catch up when there is notable job growth, so look for areas with a positive reputation, growing population, and tight vacancy rates—less than 2 per cent.

TAHANI'S TIP

When looking for prospective areas to invest in, look for areas where big box stores, such as Walmart, or large franchises, such as Starbucks, are setting up shop. These are signs that there is growth to come and that it would likely be good to buy in these areas. If Walmart or The Home Depot is moving into an area, those companies have already conducted extensive research to determine if the neighbourhood is healthy, with population on the rise and with local economic growth to support a new location.

The real estate Doppler effect

Locations adjacent to a booming area may benefit from an overflow effect and can represent good investment opportunities. For example, a large city with a boom in property values may push values up in the surrounding areas as people expand their search area for affordable housing.

Local, regional, and provincial economic climate

Taxation and jobs directly affect real estate values, so look for a business-friendly environment with minimal taxation (income and property), a fair Landlord and Tenant Law structure, and growth in new industries and jobs. The local economic development office should be "selling" the region, since this may affect the economic climate.

Infrastructure improvements and transportation expansion

Infrastructure projects and new transportation systems all point to growth. In Canada, commuter distances are measured in minutes, not kilometres, so transit projects that shorten travel time will drive home prices upward. For example, in Ontario, GO Transit recently expanded its rail service from Toronto to Barrie. This facilitated tremendous growth in what was formerly a small town on the way to cottage country. People can now live in Barrie and easily commute to Toronto. Such developments help existing towns to flourish and grow, and new communities to sprout up along the route. All of this is conducive to increasing demand for housing, which means increasing demand for rental properties in the short term and increasing property values in the long term.

> ## TOP INFRASTRUCTURE PROJECTS THAT INFLUENCE REAL ESTATE INVESTMENT
>
> - mass transit expansion
>
> - new highways and bridges
>
> - ports and rail expansion
>
> - major energy facilities
>
> - education, recreation, and medical facilities

Areas of gentrification and renewal

Areas of renewal provide the biggest potential return on investment. Look for neighbourhoods transitioning to a higher economic class—easily identifiable by the combination of older, recently renovated and newly built homes. A well-built but slightly neglected home in a prideful area is a good choice, since the area is likely poised to boom. Stick with upgrades that guarantee payback.

Diverse economy

Areas with more than one major employer generally have less volatile economies and are able to ride out the ups and downs of the real estate cycle better than towns that rely on single industries. Look for areas that have diverse and forward-looking economies based on sectors that are growing and that have solid long-term futures.

Don't look for property based purely on low prices. Many novice investors make the mistake of wanting to buy in an area because purchase prices are lower—they see a property is $200,000 in one town while a comparable home in another area is $400,000, so they think the first property must be a good deal that will yield good cash flow. In reality, however, there may be very good reasons why an area's property values are lower—and it's often because the local market fundamentals are not strong, so there may be a lot of rental vacancies or properties for sale.

Investors need to choose areas that will provide the best return for the lowest risk. Focusing on the fundamentals improves your chances for stability during the market's inevitable gyrations. You must investigate a region, its driving economic factors, and real estate demands. Focus on a town with a future: this is the first step to successful real estate investing. When analyzing the economic aspects, look at provincial or national averages, which may help identify areas that likely have strong investment opportunities, but remember that averages are generalities.

FOOD, FUEL, AND FERTILIZER

Perhaps you have heard the expression "Food, Fuel, and Fertilizer, the three *F*s that rule the world." As you do your research and due diligence on potential areas to invest in, you might want to consider towns or regions where these industries are present. They traditionally offer consistent and stable levels of employment and their tax payments benefit the community at large.

Canada is a country rich in natural resources, and with an export-based economy, many of our main trading partners are resource-poor. Since our top industries are manufacturing, services, and natural resources, our food, fuel, and fertilizers are in high demand worldwide. This means opportunity.

With an abundance of oil and natural gas, forest products, and agricultural goods, Canada is in the enviable position of being able to supply these basic needs to the world. For our industries, this translates to output, productivity, investment, and employment. The economic development and growth taking place in Alberta due to the oil sands expansion is an excellent example of this prosperity. The world needs oil, and with supply, cost, and other challenges in other petroleum-producing regions, Canada's production is in high demand.

The world also needs food, and worldwide food prices reached a record high in January 2011, according to the Food and Agriculture Organization of the United Nations. Agriculture-producing countries such as Canada are in a position to help meet—and benefit from—this long-term demand. Canadian industries and companies based in this sector have generally proven to be strong performers.

Look at the most profitable companies in Canada. Yes, you will see the obvious names such as the Royal Bank of Canada and the Bank of Nova Scotia (financial services), but you will also see Imperial Oil Limited and Enbridge Inc. (natural resources), Potash Corporation of Saskatchewan Inc. (agriculture), and Loblaw Companies Limited (food retail). Indeed, Canada is well stocked in the three Fs, so keep this in mind as you scout prospective investment locations.

As an example, consider Abbotsford, B.C. Located in the heart of the Fraser Valley about 40 kilometres east of Vancouver, it is best known historically for its agriculture, namely fresh produce, poultry, and fertilizer production. In recent years, however, it has diversified its economy into high technology and other commercial and industrial development.

Some experts think you can add a fourth F to this group: forestry. Canada is blessed with an abundance of forest resources. According to the Forest Products Association of Canada (FPAC), the sector produces $57.1 billion in goods annually and exports about $26 billion worth of production per year. More than 600,000 Canadians are directly or indirectly employed by the industry.

This is a huge industry, not just in terms of economic output but also geographic footprint. Indeed, it is truly a national industry, active in 12 of the 13 provinces and territories. Countless communities and even entire towns across Canada were quite literally built by this sector. Historic Canadian business names such as Abitibi-Price, MacMillan Bloedel, and J.D. Irving laid economic foundations in places such as Powell River, B.C., Thunder Bay, Ontario, and Saint John, New Brunswick, whose futures were long tied to the health of the forest products business.

However, historically cyclical in nature, it is also an industry that has been especially ravaged by recent economic and environmental forces. For example, Canada's newsprint producers, long among the world's largest, took a beating in the downturn that began in late 2008 when U.S. newspaper publishers, primary customers for the sector, struggled to survive. The industry has also been the subject of intense environmental pressure for decades, involving everything from its forest harvesting practices, to its use of chemicals to bleach the pulp used to make paper, to the demands to recycle more material rather than cut more trees.

As a result of these and other ongoing challenges, some of those famous Canadian business names no longer exist. They have been absorbed through mergers and acquisitions with former competitors in the United States, Scandinavia, and elsewhere, or have closed down entirely. Since 2006, according to FPAC, the industry has lost 86,900 jobs.

The industry has had to reinvent itself just to survive. No longer able to rely on its traditional production of lumber and pulp and paper, the sector now sees its future in the emerging "bio-revolution"—a burgeoning global market that reflects a growing environmental sensibility and a paradigm shift toward products that come from natural renewable sources. FPAC says Canada's forest products industry is uniquely positioned to take advantage of this new bio-economy and exploit a potential global market of about $200 billion for bio-energy, biochemicals, and bio-materials that can be extracted from trees. These products include everything from renewable fuels to lightweight plastics to non-toxic chemicals and food additives.

This is an excellent example of the importance of staying on top of developments within the economy. Here is an industry that looked to be on its knees, and while the bio-revolution doesn't necessarily represent immediate opportunity and it may take time to come to fruition (if it even happens), it's a sign that this vital Canadian sector may have a brighter future than previously thought. Towns where this industry is a major employer—and there are a lot of them across Canada—and where futures may have once looked extremely challenging, may now return to prosperity.

A note of caution: as the forest products industry example illustrates, simply having abundant resources does not guarantee perennial prosperity. As an investor, make sure any town you're considering is not dependent solely on one such sector, but has a diverse economy.

SPECIFICS, SPECIFICS, SPECIFICS

One of the most important lessons your investor-savvy agent can help you learn is that real estate markets are very specific. They are not national, provincial, or even regional. Although organizations such as the Canadian Real Estate Association, Canada Mortgage and Housing Corporation (CMHC), the Royal Bank, and others produce reports that examine real estate on a national basis and provide big-picture analyses and averages, it's important for you to drill down into specific markets.

Markets within the same province, region, or even city can vary widely. For example, Ottawa, whose economy is supported by steady government jobs, is known as a very stable market that is characterized by unspectacular but slow, steady growth. Oshawa and Windsor, on the other hand, are both dependent on the auto industry as a key local employer. When the economic downturn of late 2008 devastated the North American auto industry, they took it hard on the chin, with plant closures and layoffs. With job losses and weakened consumer confidence, it wasn't long before real estate in these towns took a serious hit as well.

Homes in those markets could be bought at drastic discounts from their recent historic norms because the economies there were reeling from the downturn. Many residents had to sell their homes and/or move elsewhere to find work. Sure, you could have bought cheap properties there, but as investments, what would you have done with them? To whom would you have rented them? To whom would you have sold them later? How would you have been able to realize positive cash flow or value appreciation?

As an investor, you need to ask: how strong are the fundamentals? When looking for a property, always look for strong fundamentals first, then for suitable areas based on the demographic needs (consider whether the area is desirable for renters and the building type is suitable for the local tenant profile, and make sure that tenants in the area will pay what you have to charge for rent), and then narrow your search to specific streets and properties.

Now that the auto industry is recovering, you may be thinking: what if I could time it right and buy in an area on the upswing? The short answer is yes, you *could* do that, but unless you're a seasoned investor with a handful of investment properties and a few years of experience behind you, such a plan is difficult and risky. You're better off sticking to a strategy based on areas with solid long-term economic fundamentals.

What if, for example, you buy in Windsor but the auto industry hits a bump on the road to recovery? What if you purchase in Oshawa and one of the plants there announces more layoffs? If you invest in towns that are dependent on one or two industries, should hard times hit, you run the risk of being at the mercy of those sectors. But if you select your prospective locations based on long-term fundamentals and diverse economies, you insulate your investment from such volatility.

That's why many investors like Ottawa. Slow, steady, and unspectacular (some would even say boring), but with a solid government-based economy, it provides something of a safe haven, free of market vacillations caused by industries going through challenging times.

Finding specific areas with all the key fundamentals—low vacancy rates, solid local economy, increasing population, and above-average job and income growth—is not easy. It takes time and energy and research, and your investor-savvy agent can guide you until you learn what to look for on your own.

One excellent source of information is CMHC—sure to become one of your new best friends once you become an investor. The *Rental Market Report*, published in June and December of each year, is some of the most important research the federal agency produces. It analyzes Canada's rental markets and provides detailed data on rents and vacancy rates, as well as on the supporting economic trends and developments.

No matter where you're looking to buy, and then rent, an investment property, research can determine which areas have the tightest rental supply, leading to greater demand—and higher rent—for your property. And it's important to remember that you must continue to stay on top of the fundamentals *once you own property*. Your job is not done when you buy a house. It's always wise to keep abreast of what's going on in the region and town you purchase in; indeed, part of your ongoing education as a sophisticated investor is to keep a close eye on the local economy and other developments. It could help determine how you manage a property or plan your exit strategy.

TAKE ADVANTAGE OF ONLINE RESOURCES

One of the great things about the Internet in the context of real estate today is that there are many excellent online resources to help you with your research and due diligence. Investors have never had it so good.

In addition to every major realtor and many individual agents maintaining their own websites, such as www.realestaterichesbook.com (check to make sure your investor-savvy realtor has one), there are those from third-party organizations such as Canada Mortgage and Housing Corporation, the Canadian Real Estate Association, financial institutions, and economic research firms. For a complete listing of suggested valuable sites, see Appendix A–Online Resources.

Here's a good example of how the power of the Internet can help you. Let's say you're considering investing in a property in Toronto, but you're not sure where, specifically. Through your research and talking with your investor-savvy agent, you know that Toronto is a top destination choice for immigrants and others moving to the province, because of everything a major city offers, particularly employment opportunities. But, with a city so vast in size and population, what areas and neighbourhoods would make solid investment choices?

Like many major cities and even some smaller municipalities, the City of Toronto operates its own website (www.toronto.ca), which contains a wealth of information that can help you in your search and due diligence. On the toronto.ca home page, input "neighbourhood profiles" in the search tool and up will pop a large selection of valuable links. One of the first will likely be "Toronto Neighbourhood Profiles," which will take you to another landing page that lists everything from general profiles and neighbourhood maps to the "Toronto Social Atlas" and descriptions of the quality of life.

Clicking on the "neighbourhood maps" link will take you to a detailed map and listing of Toronto's neighbourhoods. Click on any one of the neighbourhood links and up pops a goldmine of information: profiles of each neighbourhood by age and gender, language and ethnicity, families and dwellings, income and poverty levels, and more. Click on the profile link and you will get a PDF file with a map of the neighbourhood, showing its precise boundaries (handy, for example, in determining proximity to the lake, subway line, industrial lands, known desirable or undesirable areas, or any other landmarks) and detailed statistics. Virtually everything you could ever want to know about a neighbourhood in which you're considering buying property is right there. Of course, you should use this to augment your other research, such as comparables on properties sold, and your actual physical visits to an area.

Let's take the Toronto example one step further. Let's say you've identified a prospective investment area through your own research and the city's website, but you've seen or heard news reports about crime in the area, or you've come across similar information that concerns you. To investigate further, you can visit the website of the Toronto Police Service (www.torontopolice.on.ca). In the "Newsroom" area of the site, click on "Publications" and scroll down to "Reports." The first section is "Statistical reports," listed on an annual basis in PDF form. Much of the information is interesting, such as general staffing and operational issues within the Toronto Police Service, but perhaps not of great value in your due diligence. But look a little deeper and there are also some excellent and detailed crime statistics—on the type and frequency of crime against people and property, on a division-by-division basis—which you can then cross-reference with your neighbourhood profile information from the City of Toronto's website.

From these two resources you would be able to compile detailed and invaluable information on your prospective neighbourhood. Put it together with the other real estate–oriented research and due diligence you and your agent have conducted, and you would have a thorough understanding of city areas to help you make very well-informed decisions.

Mind you, not all towns and cities have the online resources that Toronto has. You'd be surprised, however, how much you can learn with these methods, which are there for the taking—and best of all, are free!

One final caveat: remember, every city wants to make itself sound as attractive as possible to residents, visitors, and businesses, so be aware of overly promotional information. Double-check claims and announcements whenever possible. If a town is proclaiming a company is relocating there with a new plant or office, or a new major highway is to be built, with promises of millions of dollars in investment and hundreds of jobs, try to verify the reports from other sources, such as objective media, the companies themselves, or any other government agencies involved. Not that any municipalities would deliberately mislead the public, but sometimes, for example, projects that are announced take longer than planned to come to fruition. So be diligent and discerning, and if you're basing your decision on an upcoming project or other economic development, make sure it is actually going to happen.

9 The Real Estate Cycle

If you follow the real estate market news, you no doubt have heard a lot about the real estate "bubble" over the last couple years—particularly as it pertains to the U.S. market. Worldwide economies nose-dived in late 2008, partially due to the collapse of the U.S. mortgage industry and the free fall in American real estate, from which many markets are still trying to recover.

The bubble in that market burst in catastrophic fashion, and whenever there's the slightest hiccup in the Canadian market, there's no shortage of media coverage here trumpeting similar impending doom on this side of the border. However, in the United States, the housing bubble was fuelled by sloppy lending practices that created excess demand and drove values skyward with no economic fundamentals to support them. In Canada, the federal government ensures much more stringent mortgage qualification standards and limits through its national housing agency, Canada Mortgage and Housing Corporation (CMHC). In fact, as recently as January 2011, Ottawa introduced tightened mortgage regulations—for the second time in the past 12 months.

For this reason, the type of bubble seen in the United States would probably not occur in Canada. There are no guarantees, mind you, but the Canadian mortgage framework is so closely overseen by the government and CMHC, that it is highly unlikely to occur here.

Still, it is important to understand that the real estate cycle occurs on both sides of the Canadian-U.S. border. The distinction many "experts" and others quoted in the media fail to make is that the cycles in each country are very different and, indeed, independent of one another. Many fear that, because the American market suffered a prolonged collapse, Canada's market will eventually meet the same fate. However, Canada's real estate market is very different from the U.S. real estate market, as are our respective economic and unemployment situations. While you could argue that some of Canada's largest markets—Toronto and Vancouver, for example—are overactive and face challenging conditions that may require corrections, the fact remains that the Canadian real estate market does not face the same challenges as the American market does at the moment.

Understanding these differences and knowing how the Canadian real estate cycle works are critical advantages for a Canadian investor. Working with an investor-savvy agent who has this expert knowledge and can help educate you in these areas is an invaluable asset, which can lead you to see opportunity where others see only risk.

As we discussed in Chapter 1, investor-savvy agents understand the local market and other important factors that are critical to making wise choices for investment properties. Your realtor should be an expert in the fundamentals, developments in the local economy and the local government, the vacancy and rental rates for the area, the tenant profile for the neighbourhood, and should understand what makes one potential neighbourhood or street stronger or weaker than another. And he or she should be able to explain the importance of these in the context of the real estate cycle.

For even further expert insight into the real estate cycle, we consulted Don Campbell, Kieran Trass, and Greg Head, co-authors of *Secrets of the Canadian Real Estate Cycle: An Investor's Guide*, published by John Wiley & Sons Canada, Ltd.

WHAT IS THE REAL ESTATE CYCLE?

The real estate cycle was first identified more than 70 years ago by Homer Hoyt, now regarded as the grandfather of this concept. In 1933, Hoyt analyzed a century of Chicago land values. In documenting his findings in the book *One Hundred Years of Land Values in Chicago*, Hoyt noted how a recurrent succession of causes and effects impacted land values from 1830 to 1930. He recognized a big-picture pattern at play and detailed how that pattern impacted the real estate market.

Subsequent studies support Hoyt's theory, and we now understand that the real estate cycle, also called the real estate cycle clock, follows a consistent pattern that moves through three basic stages: recovery, boom, and slump.

THE PHASES

The real estate cycle's clock can be somewhat irregular, but the fundamental pattern remains the same. In other words, the recovery, boom, and slump pattern always repeats itself, but the timeframe of each phase in the cycle is not consistent with previous cycles. The cycle is based on the simple laws of supply and demand, but if you know what factors affect these forces, the real estate cycle offers genuine predictive value. It should be one of your real estate investment fundamentals.

The Boom Phase

The boom phase tends to be the shortest phase in the real estate cycle (although anomalies do happen). During this phase, capital growth is the name of the game. There are more buyers than sellers in the market, which forces prices and property values up. This happens slowly at the start of the boom and then gathers speed as this phase progresses. The boom phase nears completion once prices reach their maximum.

During a boom, the public is very positive about buying property. High volumes and quick sales characterize this phase. Properties are snapped up soon after they go on the market, so relatively fewer listings are available for hungry purchasers.

Normally, at the start of a boom you will notice an increase in population accompanied by rising employment and income levels. Rents and property values will be going up. This means investors will be getting a greater return on investment for properties they already own. The returns on new properties are often lower at the start of a boom because increases in rent are unable to keep up with increases in property values. During the initial stages of a boom, much of the public has anti-real-estate feelings due to negative memories of the previous slump and most fail to recognize that the boom is already underway. At the same time, more people start entering the real estate market and that starts to drive property prices up.

Inexperienced investors think the boom is the time to buy properties, since we are at the peak of profitability. Little do they know that this is the time to *sell*, not buy.

During the boom, smart investors are selling their properties to take their profits and then wait for the market to shift so they can begin buying again.

By the middle of the boom, the increase in rents reaches a peak and vacancy levels are low. As the rents rise, the number of people living in each dwelling also increases since it becomes harder for people to afford to rent on their own. Values continue to rise and property sells easily and quickly. It is easy to get financing, and banks are relaxed about allowing people to borrow to the absolute maximum they can afford.

In this phase, the sellers have the negotiating power. More and more people focus on adding value to their properties and this continues until the end of the boom.

Key Boom Signs Checklist

- increasing population
- high employment
- greater income
- peaking rents
- inflated property values
- quick property sales
- easy to get financing
- more construction
- greed

The Slump Phase

In the slump phase, the increase in property values slows and the upward trend line may come to a halt as the supply of property exceeds demand. Sometimes values will erode to pre-boom levels, although this doesn't happen in every slump or in every geographic area.

This is when smart investors buy, because with property supply exceeding demand, buyers now have the negotiating edge. It takes longer to sell a property, and agents have more listings than in other phases of the real estate cycle. As fewer properties sell during a slump than at any other time, investors will notice that the same real estate agents who happily ignored them during the boom now start to return phone calls. Some of the best property-buying opportunities arise during this period, as vendors are motivated and purchasers have an extraordinary amount of control.

At the beginning of the slump phase, property values may still be rising, though at slower rates. Property sales volumes fall from their former heights and there is a lower return on investment. This is accompanied by increased holding costs, and many investors start to consider selling a property or two. The increasing number of sellers signals a further market shift, as they start competing with each other and further flooding the market with properties for sale.

Midway through a slump, there will be an abundance of motivated vendors who are forced to sell their properties due to low returns and high holding costs. The media will start to bash real estate and fear rules the day as people worry about short-term equity corrections. Employment levels are low at this stage and financing is harder to get.

As the slump nears its end, unemployment will be at its peak, population growth and incomes will be at their lowest levels, and rents will remain fairly static. By the end of the slump phase, values will be at their most affordable.

Key Slump Signs Checklist

- low to no population growth

- increasing unemployment

- decreasing incomes

- oversupply of property

- stricter financing conditions

- reduced or flat rents

- decreasing or flat property values

- desperate vendors

- fear

The Recovery Phase

As a market enters the recovery phase, the population starts to increase, resulting in a shortage of rental property. Property values begin to rise slowly, and investors start to get a better return on investment as rents rise and vacancy rates begin to fall. Interest rates are attractive and financing starts to become easier to get as banks come under pressure to lend to capitalize on the increased need for borrowing.

First-time homebuyers become more active in this market, but with memories of price corrections from the preceding slump, fear still rules. As the recovery phase progresses, experienced investors recognize the potential for increased returns and enter the market aggressively. Inexperienced investors remain cautious and most will wait to see what happens before they take any action.

The recovery period is also characterized by increased construction of new dwellings, as builders and developers start new projects. You will notice many property owners adding value to their properties at this stage in the cycle. The end of the recovery phase often blurs with the beginning of the boom, and it can be hard to tell when the cycle is changing. Throughout the recovery phase, property values will rise, but media reports will continue to reflect low investor confidence in real estate.

Key Recovery Signs Checklist

- increasing population

- new construction starts

- less restrictive financing

- rising rents

- increasing property values

- greater returns on investment

- emerging confidence in the market

How to Recognize Phase Shifts

From recovery to boom

At mid-boom, everyone from the neighbours to the taxi driver is talking about the benefits of real estate investments, as is the media. New investors enter the market, egged on by the general excitement level and an increased awareness of real estate through the media and investment seminars.

From boom to slump

Unfortunately, greed is the flavour of the month. You will notice a great deal of speculation: buyers will be buying property based on plans versus built product. As the end of the boom nears, population growth slows and the ratio of buyers to sellers starts to neutralize in the market. People also start to find it harder to meet their mortgage payments and this slows down the boom's momentum.

From slump to recovery

At the end of the slump phase, property values are low and vendors are increasingly desperate. This is the stage of the real estate cycle savvy investors have been waiting for! With very few buyers in the market at this stage, there is less competition for you as an investor. Take note of words such as "urgent" in property advertisements. In this phase, it takes longer and longer to sell properties, but you will start to see more first-time homebuyers entering the market. Even though the media is still reporting doom and gloom as far as property is concerned, these buyers are focusing in on what they can afford.

What motivates first-time homebuyers as a market moves from slump to recovery? With rents holding steady, their focus changes from asking prices to basic math. They begin to look at whether they can afford to buy a property for the same monthly payment they're already paying out as rent.

KEY DRIVERS AND MARKET INFLUENCERS

Key drivers propel the real estate market through the various phases of the cycle. Some of these drivers are volatile and others are more stable. Regardless, it is their collective impact that a real estate investor must watch.

While no single key driver can move the real estate cycle through a complete phase on its own, the right combination of drivers can have a major impact. The key drivers can be divided into three categories: demographic, financial, and emotional. An investor-savvy agent should know these indicators and be able to help you understand their importance.

Demographic

- net migration/population growth
- real estate vacancy rates
- employment
- real estate construction
- number of people per household

Financial

- real estate ROI
- rents
- incomes
- real estate finance availability
- gross domestic product
- real estate values
- real estate affordability

Emotional

- number of days to sell real estate
- gentrification
- real estate listings
- real estate sales

Demographic changes, such as population growth, can quickly increase demand for real estate. Financial drivers, such as an increase in the level of rents, can impact the financial viability of a real estate investment. An emotional driver, such as the number of days it takes to sell property, can induce panic buying when buyers are driven by the fear of missing out during the boom phase of the real estate cycle. If population growth, an increase in rent levels, and panic buying occur simultaneously, their impact on the real estate cycle is significant.

Market influencers are factors that affect the perception of the length of a specific phase of the real estate cycle. It is important to understand that market influencers are often confused with key drivers. But unlike drivers, which actually move the real estate cycle from one phase to another, market influencers impact the immediate levels of supply and demand in the real estate market. Their impact, however, is temporary.

Real estate investors need to recognize that the temporary nature of market influencers impacts the cycle by giving a false impression of where it is moving. They do not drive the real estate cycle from one phase to the next, but create the illusion of that happening. The direct result of the confusion caused by that illusion is great news for prudent investors: it can set up a window of opportunity.

Market influencers that can temporarily shift a real estate cycle include the following:

- interest rates (the cost of borrowing)

- ease of borrowing (the availability of capital)

- confidence in real estate as an investment vehicle

- inflation

- legislative amendments (taxation and/or local authority)

- investment alternatives

Understanding the real estate cycle means you can capitalize on the temporary blips created by market influencers. They often provide short-term opportunities to acquire property or execute an exit strategy.

10 Types of Investment Properties

The best types of properties can vary from location to location. For example, in downtown Kitchener-Waterloo, student housing might make a wise property selection, given the thousands of university students who populate the area. With university enrolments increasing and outpacing the space available in student residences, townhouses or multi-unit buildings close to the campuses and along transit routes are in high demand. With these properties, parking is often not a major factor because most students don't have their own vehicles, but proximity to campus is key. In contrast, regions in northern Alberta, near the oil sands, have a very different rental demographic needing a very different type of housing than the students. Tenants in that market may require shorter-term leases to accommodate seasonal work schedules or adequate parking for heavy-duty vehicles such as pickup trucks.

For first-time or novice investors, I always recommend something that is very easy to maintain—such as a townhouse or apartment condo, where the condominium corporation looks after much of the maintenance. Some novice investors want to immediately begin with a multi-family property, such as a fourplex or sixplex. However, I almost always recommend they start with something smaller until they see how comfortable they are with owning and managing a property, how much work it is, and how much time it requires. Below I discuss the most common types of investment properties.

PRE-CONSTRUCTION CONDOS

Condominiums can be bought before they're built—usually off the plan. This means purchasing after viewing only the builder's plans, marketing materials, and model suite, not the actual unit (which doesn't exist yet). Investors can sell their condo before it's complete, known as *selling your assignment clause*, which basically means you're selling your Agreement to Purchase to another buyer. More commonly, investors either sell their unit when construction is complete, often two or three years down the road, and the new owner can move into the unit, or they hold on to it and rent it out (the buy and hold strategy).

Selling upon completion has worked in some large markets, such as Toronto, in recent years, but it is risky because you can't always count on a property's value increasing sufficiently to generate a net profit over the two- or three-year construction period. In addition, depending on market conditions and how well a project sells, the condo developer may still have units of its own to sell when the building is complete or other investors may try to sell their units at the same time as you. All of this can lead to too much competition and downward pressure on pricing.

While buying pre-construction condos can be profitable in an upward market, it can also be very risky. The main challenge is that you have no idea how many other people in your building you are competing with—which makes this type of purchase more "speculating" than investing. For example, the market could decline, making your unit worth less than you paid for it. Or any number of other investors may have bought units in your building with the same hope in mind—to sell before or upon completion for a profit. If, for whatever reason, one of those investors has to sell quickly and is willing to do so at a discount, that sends the value spiralling downward for all other investor-owned units in the building (including yours).

Don't—*do not*—line up to buy a pre-construction unit. Most buyers who do so are "emotional investors," at the mercy of market fluctuations and the intentions of others. These people are not smart investors, who buy on the basis of fundamentals and a well-thought-out strategy. Think about it: when you line up in a crowd of hundreds of other buyers to purchase a pre-construction unit, your emotions—and the builder's sales pitch—take over. Once you get into the sales office, you're often told the prices have already increased, so you're encouraged to act now! Buy now or lose out on the opportunity! Don't be one of those who buys on emotion. Be a smart businessperson.

RESALE PROPERTIES

For novice investors, a much safer route is to buy resale properties. You know what you're buying—it already exists—what it can rent for, and what the local rental demographic is.

I almost always advise my clients to buy resale. Indeed, the model of the Real Estate Investment Network is to look for properties that are 20 to 40 years old, because these existing homes are typically in established neighbourhoods. There may be some work required to increase their value, but these homes are likely less expensive to buy than new homes in the same area, and can generate sufficient rental income—against a lower purchase price and mortgage—to deliver positive cash flow. And remember, your goal as a buy and hold investor is cash flow, cash flow, cash flow.

For example, let's say a client comes to me having identified a solid prospective neighbourhood. A new townhouse in the area may cost $250,000, but a 30-year-old semi only costs $180,000. The older semi may command a little less rent than the new townhouse, and it may require more maintenance. The mortgage on the new property would be much higher, making the cash-flow ratio superior to that of the semi.

There are always advantages and disadvantages to weigh with every property. This is why it's important to base your decisions on the fundamentals, do the due diligence, and see what makes the best case as an investment.

When you apply this strategy to buying a finished product in an existing neighbourhood, you already know the area, you've worked the numbers, and you know the cash-flow potential of a property. Isn't that better than buying with more hope than research and knowledge, basing your decision on pre-construction marketing, and competing against other investors who may have no idea what they're doing?

SECONDARY SUITES

Many investors come to me looking for a house with a basement apartment in it, or the potential to add one, thinking that the additional revenue stream will help generate more income and positive cash flow. Such a plan can work well if the rent generates revenue to help cover the mortgage and carrying costs.

Municipal law governs the regulations on secondary suites, so it's critical that investors and their agents examine the local bylaws—*before* purchasing a property. In the Kitchener-Waterloo region of Ontario, for example, a home with a secondary suite is considered a duplex, and must be legally recognized as such by the municipality.

These bylaws vary from location to location; don't assume that just because secondary suites are legal in one part of town that they also are in another. Investors considering this strategy should always check each situation with the local municipality *beforehand* to determine if adding a suite can be done and if any rezoning is necessary (often a lengthy process that can take months). I have heard stories from investors who counted on the additional income from a secondary suite when they bought homes, but then couldn't get the zoning approved—and the purchase was a done deal. A very costly mistake.

While properties with secondary suites are appealing, there are numerous challenges in adding one. For example, if you buy a detached home on a street with other similar detached homes owned by primary buyers, and you apply for rezoning to convert the basement into a rental apartment, your neighbours have a voice in that application process—and they may oppose your plan. If the home is located on an exclusive street with affluent residents, and rentals are not common in the area, people may object out of fear that a basement apartment on the property may negatively affect property values, or that it may lead to more traffic on the street and parking concerns. On the other hand, if the property is in a neighbourhood close to rental apartments, or if other houses on the street have basement apartments, there may be no objections and your application may sail through the approval process.

There is usually a small fee to apply for rezoning, but the cost of application is not the issue—it's the cost of retrofitting the house for a secondary suite. Most critically, such modifications must meet proper building codes for items such as ceiling height, exits and entrances, and other essentials. One of my clients had to take down the basement ceiling and re-strap it because it was one inch lower than the height mandated by the building code—*one inch*. Imagine the work, cost, and time required to redo such a job if it fails inspection.

For anyone considering adding a secondary suite illegally—stop right there. It's not worth the risk. There are liability issues regarding your tenants, and insurance concerns for the property itself, not to mention the possibility that the home may be difficult to resell. There is also the risk that the municipality could come in at any moment and shut down your business, leaving you with no additional income from your secondary unit to carry the property costs.

TAHANI'S TIP

When you see an advertisement for a house with a secondary suite, always visit the planning department at the appropriate municipality to check for yourself if it is legally zoned. Don't assume that it is.

However, when done properly, secondary suites can work well. Adding a legal secondary suite after you buy a home can raise its value and generate additional income to help pay the mortgage and other costs. Remember: the key considerations are the time required for any rezoning application, and the time and capital costs for the renovation itself. When you take all that into account, you can then decide if it's worth buying a property and adding a suite, or buying one that has the zoning or a suite itself in place already.

Note: You cannot go through the rezoning application process until *after* you've bought the property. Therefore, it's essential that you know the municipal regulations before you purchase so you know what you'll be facing. Some people think, "Oh, let's put an offer on a house with a condition on getting the rezoning approved." Well, why would any seller want to wait six months or longer for that process to play itself out? The short answer is: most sellers wouldn't.

When you're looking at a property with the idea of adding a secondary suite, in most cases you can't use the revenue from a basement apartment as a source of income when you apply for a mortgage, because you're buying it as a single-family home. If the property has an *existing* suite with a tenant under lease, that's a different story, because it's proven, verifiable income. Otherwise, most lenders won't give you mortgage application credit for potential rent from a future and currently unapproved secondary suite.

TAHANI'S TIP

Bylaws governing secondary suites differ between provinces and municipalities, so you or your investor-savvy agent should always check with the authorities—before you buy.

GUEST COMMENTARY

Adding a secondary suite

By Cindy Wennerstrom, Oro Properties, Toronto, Ont.

Adding a secondary suite to an investment property is a brilliant way to achieve additional cash flow. However, there are many important considerations. Is the home capable of housing a secondary suite? At what cost? Does the new set-up of the home meet all safety requirements according to the local fire code? And finally, is the home legally zoned for two suites?

With each consideration there are pros and cons. Almost any home has the potential to be renovated—you just need a creative eye to see the best option for the second suite. Most people believe a basement is the only plausible area for a secondary suite, but another option is to split the home so the upstairs becomes the secondary suite. Or perhaps the split works best in the middle of the home so the apartments are split as main floor/basement and main floor/upper level. There are often several options.

Sometimes, the layout depends on existing plumbing or proximity and access to electrical, which can substantially reduce renovation costs. And these costs are often difficult to estimate; budget about 20 per cent of the total cost as a buffer, as you are certain to run into issues and unexpected or desired upgrades. Generally speaking, a full kitchen (IKEA-style) with regular countertops, new sink and faucet, and stainless appliances purchased through a wholesale club, reclamation store, or "scratch and dent" store will run $4,000 to $5,000. A wall to separate the spaces with sound insulation, resilient channel, fire-rated drywall, and fresh paint will cost approximately $2,000. Flooring, if necessary, will run between $1,500 and $3,000, depending on the size of the unit and flooring selected. A full four-piece bathroom with tiles and new fixtures will cost about $5,000. Building, electrical, and plumbing permits, along with architectural drawings, will add about $2,500 to the project's cost.

Any unit you rent *must* be safe, so you need to ensure it meets all fire-code standards. The local fire department can confirm this, or you can hire a company that specializes in offering advice and providing certificates once the work has been completed. Generally, these companies are operated by former fire marshals who are well versed in what you'll need to do. One of the best safety features you can build in is interconnected smoke alarms on all floors. If one alarm sounds, all the alarms will sound, alerting residents in both units to a potential fire. Also, ensure that fire-rated drywall, sound insulation, and resilient channel are used for any walls or ceilings that are shared between units.

Once you find a home and determine it's suitable to split into separate units, have an architect draw the plans and submit them to the appropriate municipality for a permit to legally become a duplex— and make sure the home is legally zoned for two suites. In Toronto, for example, most homes are allowed to have two units, as long as they meet some basic requirements with respect to ceiling heights, windows, entrances, exits, and parking. The City of Toronto, for instance, requires a parking spot for each unit.

Rules and laws governing secondary suites differ between municipalities, so it's important to do your homework before getting your heart set on a specific area or property.

The process can be cumbersome, lengthy, and sometimes expensive, and consequently many people decide to split a home into a duplex *without* permits. This is not advisable. Permits ensure that your contractors build to the proper code, which protects you should there be any problems or accidents in the future. Furthermore, when it comes time to sell, you can say with confidence that your home meets all zoning laws and building and electrical codes. This is a definite selling feature and could help produce a higher selling price.

TIPS

- Budget 20 per cent of your renovation costs as a buffer for unforeseen expenses.

- Interconnect fire alarms on all floors.

- Use fire-rated drywall and sound insulation for any walls or ceilings that are shared between units.

COMMERCIAL REAL ESTATE

Investing in commercial real estate is quite different from investing in residential property. I don't recommend it for novice investors, but once you're a seasoned investor with several years of experience and a number of deals behind you, it's an option you may choose to pursue. Commercial real estate involves buying multi-family residences with five or more units or commercial retail spaces, whose tenants are typically businesses, such as medical and law offices, restaurants, spas, small retailers, and any number of other professional services.

GUEST COMMENTARY

Investing in commercial multi-family properties (five or more units)

By Pierre-Paul Turgeon, president, Matterhorn Real Estate Investments Ltd., Calgary, Alta.

Multi-family housing is a form of residential property investing that has more than one unit in the same building. Within multi-family properties there are two basic categories:

- small multi-family properties, which are buildings with one to four units and are considered residential investments

- large multi-family properties, which are buildings with five or more units and are considered commercial investments

Lending institutions created the four-unit cut-off to distinguish between properties that individuals may purchase as their primary residences (the owner may or may not live in one of the suites) and properties that are acquired strictly as income investment vehicles. CMHC, for instance, includes small rental properties in its homeownership products category, whereas properties with five or more units are categorized as "multi-unit properties," also often referred to as "commercial multi-family properties." Each category of property has a completely different set of financing rules.

There are many valid reasons why real estate investors may wish to invest in commercial multi-family properties of five or more units. For example, investors who own several small rental properties may find that managing them is too labour-intensive. Owning multi-unit buildings can allow investors to manage a real estate business of similar value all under one roof, so to speak. Another reason is that the federal government has recently implemented measures that restrict the number of small investment properties investors can purchase using mortgage-default insurance offered by CMHC. Once investors hit that ceiling, they can no longer leverage their income and buy more properties using the same method.

Investors shaken by the recent economic downturn in the stock market are now looking for less risky investments such as multi-family properties. In the last two years, investors have realized that commercial apartment buildings are very stable and low-risk investments. In fact, Moody's Investor Service, an organization that assigns independent rating opinions to help investors assess credit risk, ranked the multi-family rental market at 99 points out of 100. This score is the strongest among all property types measured by Moody's.

Throughout the recession, apartment buildings held their value and there were no distress sales, since owners were able to easily refinance their debt through CMHC at very low interest rates. This meant they were able to obtain refinancing and withdraw large amounts of equity to pay down other debts or make other investments, such as buying more real estate—and do so at a time when debt markets were pretty much closed for other types of investments.

Other advantages of investing in commercial multi-family properties include:

- greater creation of long-term wealth

- more efficient use of your time—and more time to yourself if you decide to hire a professional property manager who is paid out of the property's income

- less capital required—you may be able to purchase properties with as little as 15 per cent down (versus 25 per cent on conventional lending)

- potential for greater cash flow—if your property is well managed and bought at the right price

- no consideration of your personal income—as long as the property provides positive cash flow

- no limit—as long as each property cash-flows sufficiently, an investor can purchase any number of properties

- consolidation of operating expenses—all under one roof as opposed to being spread out among different smaller properties that produce smaller profits

- reduced vacancy impact—when you own multiple units versus a single home

- better economies of scale—having larger properties can lead to cost savings

On the down side, investing in commercial multi-family properties presents investors with some significant challenges that cannot be overlooked. For one, there are fewer properties and fewer players/sellers at this level, including fewer realtors, mortgage brokers, and banks specializing in multi-family properties. Accordingly, you quickly develop a reputation in this business, which you have to protect at all costs if you wish to continue buying multi-family properties in the future.

Another major hurdle is that these properties require greater capital resources up front than small multi-family properties. That includes not only the initial down payment, but also meeting the minimum personal net worth requirement of 25 per cent of the loan amount if it is CMHC-insured. For example, if you take a loan for $2 million, you need to have a minimum net worth of $500,000 in order to qualify as a borrower. In addition, investors need to factor in significant financial contingencies. For example, if the boiler for a 30-apartment building bursts, it will be much more expensive to replace than the furnace in a single-family rental property. Lastly, borrowers also need to provide personal guarantees of up to 50 per cent of the loan amount if it's CMHC-insured. For a $2 million loan, if the loan-to-value is at the maximum of 85 per cent, the borrower would have to provide a personal guarantee of $1 million.

As a result of being considered low risk and profitable over time, apartment buildings are currently in high demand, and their supply is dwindling in Canada. Recent national data indicates that vacancy rates in apartment buildings are at near-record lows, but expensive land and high construction costs are keeping developers from building new inventory. Accordingly, despite the high demand for commercial multi-family properties, the supply remains low and it can be very difficult to find buildings to purchase.

For more information: www.matterhorninvesting.com

GUEST COMMENTARY

Investing in commercial retail plaza properties

By Mike Cunning, Upcountry Group, North Vancouver, B.C.

There are some key differences between investing in retail commercial and residential real estate. For one thing, no one lives in a retail commercial property—meaning the tenant is a *business*, not a person or family. Businesses make money, or at least generate revenue, against which they must pay expenses, one of which is rent to the commercial landlord.

A central benefit to commercial investing is something that doesn't exist in residential real estate—the triple net lease, also known as NNN or 3N. This is a lease in which the tenant pays the rent, as well as all taxes, insurance, and maintenance expenses. So, for example, if the municipal government raises the local property, water, and sanitary taxes, all of those costs are borne by the tenant, not the owner-landlord. In a residential lease, the landlord is usually responsible for everything but the rent.

Long-term tenancy is also an important difference with commercial real estate, since the tenants tend to put down roots and build their businesses once they settle on a location. This, in turn, provides stability for the owner-landlord, since if a business is doing well and making money, presumably it can continue to pay the rent and other expenses to the landlord.

Another key difference is that a commercial landlord has very clear rights if a tenant doesn't pay rent. Again, the tenant is a business, not a person or family, so landlord control and eviction processes are simple and clear-cut. If a tenant doesn't pay the rent, it is easier to evict them. With residential real estate, if a tenant doesn't pay rent, you can still evict them, but depending on the province and municipality and the corresponding landlord-tenant regulations, it can be a long and arduous process.

Because commercial properties are income-producing businesses, they are easier to value than residential properties. Given this fact, loan-to-value ratios are usually much lower; accordingly, vendor financing is more readily accepted than with residential properties.

Pluses of commercial real estate

- No one lives in it!

- Tenancies are longer and usually more stable—doctors and dentists are great tenants.

- Operating expenses and taxes are recoverable under triple net leases.

- Commercial property is much easier to manage than residential.

Minuses of commercial real estate

- Vacancies are usually longer and require the landlord to provide incentives to induce tenants.

TIPS

- The triple net lease is your friend.

- Commercial real estate is less hands-on.

- Start small and walk before you run. Buy a small plaza, learn by doing, and expand from there. Don't run out and buy a 30,000-square-foot building. Take your lumps on something small.

Viewing Investment Properties

As we have discussed, your decisions should be anchored by the economic fundamentals of your prospective investment area, as well as your financial situation and level of experience. Once you have identified a region to invest in, you can then narrow your search down to a specific town—say, looking at the Region of Waterloo in Ontario, then the town of Cambridge. Then, from the town level, you can zero in even further to a specific neighbourhood and street.

Novice investors shouldn't get too hung up on a specific *style* of property and how nice the area is. It's more important to look at what type of tenant you want to attract and how much a property can rent for—based on your research of the area and the tenant profile. Answering those questions first will determine the best type of property—meaning that most desired by renters in the area—to look at.

If you want a professional type of tenant because that's what you've identified as the rental demographic for an area, a suitable property might be a detached home. I have an investment property in Cambridge that is a detached home with a two-car garage, and it's always rented to executives. In another area, the tenant profile might be more working-class, in which case an appropriate property might be a semi-detached home or townhouse, since affordability is usually a key factor for these tenants.

Your goal, remember, is to become an expert in the local market, with an understanding of the housing types and the tenant profiles. The east part of a town, for example, could be very different from the west, and within those areas, the neighbourhoods and streets could vary widely as well.

One thing you *don't* want is to be in an area with a lot of speculative buyers—such as those "investors" buying pre-construction condos that we discussed earlier. It's too risky to have the success of your investment affected by inexperienced and unsophisticated investors who may not know how to make smart real estate investment decisions.

In addition to looking for an area with solid economic fundamentals, you want to find a neighbourhood that is attractive to your desired tenant profile, with proximity to amenities such as shopping malls, recreation and health care facilities, transit routes, and highways, and with potential for growth. Major infrastructure improvements, such as new roads and transportation projects, are key influences on property values—which is important to you as an investor—and are also major attractions for your tenants.

After choosing the area you want to invest in and defining your tenant profile, we come to your next important decision: the type of housing. Keep in mind, cash flow is king, so your price range (determined primarily by how much money you have as a down payment) will help determine the type of housing to buy. In the area you've identified as having strong potential, what type of housing is most desired by the tenant profile? Single detached homes? Semi-detached or townhouses? Duplexes? Condos? Of the most desired properties, which can you afford and which will provide you the most cash flow?

Remember, your goal is to buy a cash-flowing property that will appreciate in value. If you have done your due diligence and examined the fundamentals, and have determined you can generate positive cash flow by buying a semi and renting to a tenant you feel comfortable with, that's a solid strategy. Don't become set on buying a specific property type, such as a detached home, without knowing who you might be able to rent it to and for how much.

HOW MANY PROPERTIES TO LOOK AT?

Is there a magic number for how many properties you should look at? This is a great question. Is there a strategy to looking? Most expensive to least expensive? In random order? This is another area where your investor-savvy agent can prove their value, making the answers to these questions a lot simpler than you may think.

By this point, working together, the two of you have already identified a strong area and neighbourhood, your price range, the desired property type, and the approximate rent. By the time you're reviewing listings of potential properties, you should already know, based on your down payment and other basic information, how much cash flow can be generated. After eliminating those properties that don't provide an appropriate amount of cash flow, you can focus on considerations such as the condition of a property, how much work it might require to make it market-ready, or simple improvements that would allow you to charge more rent and, therefore, generate higher cash flow. This is why it's important to work with an investor-savvy realtor—to save you both time and energy and, ultimately, money.

So, let's go back to the question: how many properties? Every investor's situation and personality type is different. For some, all they need is to see that the numbers work and they buy the first time I take them out. Others are a little more deliberate and need to see a number of houses before they feel comfortable enough to take action.

For example, I met a client (let's call him Max) and within one meeting and two phone calls, we figured out what Max wanted. I then booked three properties for him to see with his wife. Well, Max ended up buying two out of the three. He knew what he wanted, he understood the area, he did a lot of work before looking at the properties, and he knew they would generate good cash flow. It could turn out that you are like Max, that you like and buy the very first house you look at. The more you know an area, and the more skilled you become at scouting properties, the fewer units you need to view.

Another example is Jack. Jack and I went through the same preparation process as Max and I did. I took Jack out to see many properties over the course of a year before he felt ready to buy—which was fine, because investors go at their own pace. Over that year, however, he saw purchase prices and rents in the area increase. I encouraged him to step forward and take action. *Fear* was stopping him, not the prospective investments themselves.

Inexperienced investors, or those working with inexperienced agents, can look at a dozen or more properties, because they don't really know what they're looking for. For most investors I work with, we look at three to five properties, and rarely more, because we have narrowed down the search beforehand. I suggest properties that I *know* fit my client's strategy, and that I *know* will generate sufficient positive cash flow.

It is important to work the numbers (see the Property Analyzer in Appendix D) on prospective properties before you physically go out looking at them. Unless you happen to be buying in the same town you live in, viewing potential houses will likely involve some travel, so save yourself and your agent a lot of time, headaches, and frustration by doing the math in advance.

After visiting each property, it's important to conduct a brief "post-mortem" and analyze why you didn't buy it, what you liked and didn't like, and what you need to do differently before looking at another unit. Doing this after viewing every property helps to clarify what you want and to find the right investment next time.

If clients don't seem ready to buy by the third time out, I begin to wonder why. Again, they're not buying a home to live in, but an investment property—judged by a completely different set of criteria. If we have done our homework—identified a strong area, a solid neighbourhood and street, the tenant profile, and the rental rate, and have selected potential properties that will produce positive cash flow—the decision is much easier than buying a primary home. There's no emotional component to the investment property buying equation, no waiting to fall in love with a home. This is a business, and we should know exactly what we're looking for.

VISIT BEFORE YOU BUY

Step number one, and an important lesson to hammer home here: always visit a property before you buy—never, ever buy a property sight unseen, no matter how good a deal it seems to be. It may sound obvious, but you should walk the land and see the property first-hand to get a feel for the building, its immediate environment, and the surrounding neighbourhood.

Don't be like some of the investors I have met who bought property in the United States or elsewhere just because someone told them it was a good deal. When they actually went south to look at the property, they found out what a disastrous deal they had made. The area was awful, and they just couldn't sell the property. They made the big mistake of not looking first, and it's costing them thousands and thousands of dollars.

Remember, your checklist for strong prospective properties includes:

- located in an area of strong fundamentals
- reasonable purchase price
- desirable for renters who fit the local demographic
- must always provide positive cash flow

You and your investor-savvy realtor should identify a reasonable target of a few potential properties to physically visit. Once you begin to look at individual homes, you can finalize your choice using a different, more property-focused, set of criteria.

Location

Before you even get to the property, you should have a good understanding of the general location vis-à-vis proximity to appealing features such as shopping, schools, mass transit, and other amenities. But when you're actually on-site, this is your first opportunity to stand on the grounds and get a feel for the intangibles that you don't always find on listing information sheets or in the comparables prepared by your realtor.

Start by viewing the outside of a property, examining the general condition of the structure, the site, and any adjacent properties and land. For example, is it near an undesirable property, be it another residence or even a commercial or industrial building? Or is the property close to a busy and noisy street or intersection? If families are your target demographic, this may not be conducive to renting to them.

Property condition

Even your own casual inspection, which is not intended to replace a professional inspection (more on this later), may reveal areas of concern, such as broken or ill-fitting doors and windows, roofing, or eaves. If it's an older property, are there any necessary repairs, and at what cost?

Neighbours

Even if the property isn't a condo, semi, or other kind of property where neighbours are immediately close by, check the surrounding neighbourhood to make sure it aligns with what your target rental profile will want. Are the residents a similar age to your target renter demographic? If you hope to rent to families, is the street safe for children? And, importantly, will the surrounding properties somehow affect the value of your own unit, either positively or negatively?

Parking

Is there adequate parking for your tenants? And is there parking available nearby for visitors?

Common space

If the property is a condo, townhome, or even a semi-detached home, there may be common space that is shared by residences. As an owner, what would your associated costs be, say, for maintenance fees in a condo? If it's a semi and there's a shared driveway, what condition is it in and do the residents of the adjoining unit seem like reasonable, co-operative neighbours?

Interior

Once you've examined the exterior of a property, you can then tour the interior, paying attention to items such as the design, condition and size of the property, and how well it might fit the needs of your desired tenant.

Remember, you're purchasing the property as an investment, not as your own home, so there's no need to worry about it matching your personal tastes. You may be able to tell just from its appearance how well a home has been cared for and maintained (though a good cleaning and some paint can temporarily cover up neglect). Are there things in an obvious state of disrepair, such as windows, doors, closets, cupboards, and kitchen or bathroom plumbing? If so, are these minor fixes or major, costly repairs? Is there anything about the interior that may indicate why a property is for sale at its current asking price, such as structural damage or problems with any of the operating systems such as wiring? If the property is a condo or semi-detached, how does the condition of any adjoining or adjacent units compare, and how might that affect your unit?

Of course, you may be able to spot the obvious things, but this part of the process is where you need to call on another valuable member of your team—a qualified professional home inspector. A home inspector examines a property's condition and operating systems—everything from the structure itself to the roofing, the furnace, the plumbing and electrical, and the windows.

Take heed: do not scrimp on this part of the process. To save a little money, don't make the mistake of using a friend or your handy Uncle Fred instead of an experienced, qualified inspector. Uncle Fred may be a handyman, and he may be nice and tell you only good things about a prospective property, but for the sake of a small fee, say $350 to $500, a professional inspector will provide peace of mind. After all, this is what they do for a living; they know the hidden things to look for, concerns that can't always be seen by the naked eye, such as foundation issues, faulty wiring, aging plumbing, or mould.

Remember, standards and accreditation regulations in this occupation vary widely between provinces, so be diligent when you're checking inspectors' qualifications. This is another key area where your investor-savvy agent will prove valuable, with referrals to people they have worked with successfully in the past. (I always look for home inspectors who are also engineers.)

Occasionally, an inspector may uncover an issue that requires the attention of another type of specialist. For example, mould can be one of the worst hidden defects of a property: it can be covered up by paint, carpeting, or other cosmetic upgrades, while the actual cause of the problem may still exist.

In such cases, an inspector may recommend that a mould specialist assess the situation to get a detailed, accurate read of the problem. Likewise, he may suggest an electrician look at the wiring or a plumber inspect the piping or water systems—the same way that your doctor, a general practitioner, may refer you to a specialist for a health matter that requires expert attention. Beyond a more accurate assessment of the problem, and more importantly, specialists can provide a detailed estimate of repair costs—which should be in writing for anything major.

If you view a property and are seriously interested, your realtor could prepare an offer conditional on the home successfully passing inspection by a qualified inspector.

If the inspection uncovers something that needs repair, you can go back to the seller and ask them if they're willing to pay for all or part of it, depending on the specifics, or you could negotiate a suitable reduction of the purchase price.

TAHANI'S TIPS

- Always look at the outside of the property first, considering location and proximity to things that are desirable—and undesirable.

- When repairs or renovations are needed on a property, always get a written estimate.

- When major work is necessary, hire a specialist (for example, plumber, electrician, foundation or mould specialists).

- Always write offers with a "condition on inspection," even if you don't want to exercise this option.

CASE STUDY: HIDDEN DEFECTS CAN BE HAZARDOUS TO YOUR HEALTH

Here's a story I want you to remember.

An agent in Kitchener-Waterloo-Cambridge had a listing in my area and brought a couple from Toronto to view the property. It was located in a good neighbourhood, had recently been renovated, showed extremely well, was clean and bright, and everything looked great. The couple loved the home, put in an offer and bought it.

Everything was fine until they had a baby girl. When the child was about six months old, she began showing mysterious rashes. Doctors eventually diagnosed the cause as allergies, most likely attributed to mould.

"What mould?" the couple asked, in understandable disbelief. "We don't have mould. The house is great, and there are no signs of mould anywhere."

Fast-forward a year or so, and the couple became my clients. I went to visit them at the house, and they began telling me the story of their baby's mould-related illness. My heart stopped—not only out of concern for the child, but because I *remembered* this property.

The previous owner had asked me to help him sell it a couple of years back, but there were problems with the flooring, with leaky plumbing causing water damage, and other issues. I refused to sell it the way it was. As a realtor, I have a responsibility to conduct my business with honesty and integrity, and I could not in good conscience list this property for sale, pretending everything was okay with it. If I did so, it could come back to haunt me later in terms of damage to my reputation or, worse, liability. I refused, unless the problems were professionally repaired.

The owner, too cheap to spend the money on professional trades, must have made cosmetic improvements to the property in order to facilitate a sale—with this other agent—but he failed to *repair* the problems.

This poor couple ended up buying the home, not knowing mould was growing behind the walls and under the carpet their baby played on daily. Their daughter is now having serious respiratory issues, requiring expensive treatments and medication. They tried to repair the problem, but the mould eventually resurfaced. The couple has since bought and is moving into another house.

You want to know the real kicker to this story? The mouldy property actually passed inspection when it was first sold! Clearly, this raises questions about the qualifications of the home inspector, and underlines the importance of using professional, trustworthy, and recommended team members, and of course, the value of having an agent with local market expertise.

DETERMINING THE VALUE OF A PROPERTY

You can use three different approaches to determining the value of a property.

Note: Use a combination of these methods to try to determine value as accurately as possible.

1. **Comparative Market Analysis (CMA):** This is the approach most commonly used by realtors to find the value of a property. Realtors use the MLS® to find information on similar homes, including ones for sale currently, recently sold, or whose listings have expired. They start by comparing other homes in the area based on criteria such as square feet, the number of bedrooms and bathrooms, whether there's a garage

or finished basement, age of the furnace and roof, and so on. Matching these factors, a realtor will look for similar sold and active listings in the area, and then narrow it down to the same street—or search by street first, and then expand the scope to the neighbourhood until they find suitable comparables. Because it's rare to find two identical properties for sale, they make some adjustments to create a fair price comparison. For example, if House A has a garage and House B does not, they may estimate $10,000 more for House A with a single-car garage. But if House B has a finished basement and House A does not, then House B is worth $20,000 more than House A. Factoring both of these considerations into the estimate, House B is worth $10,000 more than House A.

2. **Cost approach:** This method is often used by real estate appraisers, most commonly when vacant land is being sold and the appraiser is estimating what it would cost to build a property. If a buyer is building new homes on a lot, then the cost approach is used, with adjustment for factors such as use (zoning, size, location, and features for the property). The limitation of this approach is that depreciation (when the value of a property declines) might be difficult to estimate accurately. In addition, construction costs vary, depending on location, supply and demand, and inflation, making the cost approach valuation more of an estimate.

3. **Income approach:** This method is important for investors and is most commonly used when trying to determine the value of an income property. It assumes that the value of the property is dependent on the income it produces right now, not in the future. Factors that affect this approach include the mortgage interest rate, taxes, rent control, inflation, cost of supply and demand, plus the other factors used in the CMA method—type of property, age of the building, whether it's metered separately for utilities, and the location and general area.

CAP (capitalized) rate, ROI (return on investment), and NOI (net operating income) are used to determine the value of the property. For example, to determine the CAP rate of a property, you will use this formula:

I = income (or ROI)

R = rate (CAP)

V = value or fair market value (FMV)

The formula goes like this: $I = R \times V$.

If you pay $250,000 for an income property and you are looking for a 7 per cent return on your investment, what net operating income would be required? The answer is $I = R \times V$ or $7\% \times \$250,000 = \$17,500$. You would need a net operating income of $17,500.

If you need to determine the CAP rate, you use $R = I$ divided by $V \times 100\%$ or $\$17,500/\$250,000 \times 100\% = 7\%$. Therefore, as an investor, you will earn 7 per cent return on your $250,000 investment (ROI).

If you are looking for the value of the property and you know the I and R, then use the following formula to calculate the amount you should pay: $V = I$ divided by R or $\$17,500/7\% = \$250,000$.

Another important consideration is the number of listings in the area: are there a lot of houses for sale, and if so, why? What's going on in the area? Concerns could be anything from soil contamination to an industrial plant or hydro transmission line too close to a residential area. You must always be thinking and asking those kinds of critical questions.

Should you rely on yourself or your realtor to determine the value of a property? The answer is: rely on both. And for sure, never solely on your agent. Always remember that you are the CEO of your company. Ask your realtor lots of questions, request CMAs on all properties under consideration—but you are ultimately in charge.

Another point of caution is to not wait for the deal of the century before you buy. As long as you're serious about your strategy and your plan, and you do your research and due diligence, taking action is usually better than falling prey to "paralysis by analysis." By waiting for the deal of a lifetime—which I can tell you is exceedingly rare—you may miss out on a number of excellent opportunities with great potential.

As an investor-buyer, you're not looking to take advantage of sellers or even looking for outstanding deals. Because you're focused on the long term, even average deals that are fair for both parties are sufficient, since, with your strategy, time will help produce the benefit and deliver the value of the investment.

The beauty of becoming a sophisticated investor and knowing what to look for in prospective investment towns and properties is that once you find such areas, you and your investor-savvy agent can then become experts in that local market, and you can invest in future properties there. You can repeat the process over and over again. If you've identified a strong area that affords you solid, cash-flowing property selections, why not stay and buy your next unit there? No need to reinvent the wheel every time out, right?

TAHANI'S TIPS

- Ask, ask, and ask critical questions about prospective investment areas.

- Do your research *before* you begin your property search.

- Know the cash-flow potential of each property—before you physically look at it.

- Get your agent to prepare a CMA on any property you're seriously interested in.

- It's not how many properties you see that determines when to buy, it's the quality of the investment and the cash flow.

- Never rely only on your agent. This is your business and you are the CEO.

GUEST COMMENTARY

The power of your realtor adopting your investment strategy

By Joe Ragona, JDR Investments, Oakville, Ont.

Using a realtor who is also an investor is one of the best decisions any investor can make. Such realtors understand your purpose and that you are looking at properties in a completely different way than a regular buyer. They will look for properties in your chosen area that attract your desired tenant profile and will fit your exit strategy later on.

As a savvy investor, you do not want to waste time visiting properties that do not fit your overall plan. For example, I look for long-term (five to seven years) holds with at least $100 of monthly positive cash flow in areas of potential growth that, through economic development, will be higher than the anticipated national average.

My investor-savvy agent provides the necessary information such as neighbourhood demographics and rental and vacancy rates. I then use this information to analyze the potential of a property, using very conservative numbers and inflated expenses. This way, I protect myself from market fluctuations.

Buying properties that fit your strategy is key. I target areas that are projected to appreciate quickly, allowing me to pull out equity equal to my initial investment as soon as possible so I can pursue new opportunities, while the remaining asset becomes self-sustaining. My plan is to continue to add assets that are easy to sell later and that are attractive to first-time buyers or empty nesters.

For novice investors, buying properties that appeal to your target market is also key, so it is important to know to whom you want to rent. Then, have your realtor find the best place to attract those tenants.

I trust my agents' judgment and experience when they bring properties to me. If I have done my homework in educating them about what I want to achieve, then they will bring me opportunities that only fit my investment plan. My realtors focus on unearthing such deals in my areas of interest and negotiating the deals on my behalf. Their skill, knowledge, and time are precious, and I respect these qualities. They are "in the trenches" every day, and if the market shifts, they will tell me.

You should also have your exit strategy planned out before buying—even if it's five to ten years out. This is extremely important, over and above just having the cash-flow numbers work. How will you get your money out of this investment? If you sell, who will buy it—first-time buyers, your tenant, empty nesters? Or is it only attractive to other investors or a niche market such as executives?

When analyzing properties, remember to include major expenses and to factor in any pricing fluctuations for the future. As mentioned above, I use conservative income and inflated expense estimates to begin my analysis; if that works, then I know the real numbers will look even better.

Novice investors can benefit from knowing their plan in advance and by choosing a realtor who adopts the same plan and brings them the exact opportunities to help them achieve their goals.

12

Negotiating the Offer

The best part of being an investor, and your strength at the negotiating table, is that you're not buying properties to live in as your primary residence. They are investments, intended to make money, pure and simple. The financials either work or they don't. And when you look at potential deals with this frame of mind, you are able to be—and *need* to be—less emotionally attached to purchases. There are no "Oh, I love this house and I must have it" moments. This translates into tremendous power for investors, if used properly.

YOUR UNIQUE NEGOTIATING POSITION

As an investor, you can be very flexible when you write offers. You may be able to close on a deal quickly, as opposed to primary home buyers who have to sell their existing house first, secure financing, and so on. A seller needing a fast sale might be looking for exactly the buying power and agility you possess, which could mean a better deal for you, the buyer. This can also work the other way around. If the seller is looking for a long closing, you can offer this as well, and still get a great deal because of the flexibility and peace of mind you're providing the seller.

For example, if an investor-client of mine likes a property and wants to submit an offer, we can prepare two very different proposals at the same time:

- One offer might be for a fair price, but include a request for vendor financing (also known as a vendor take-back mortgage, in which the seller provides some or all of the mortgage financing, depending on the size of the deal) in order to facilitate the sale.

• The other offer scenario might be for less money, but with straight-forward financing from a traditional lender.

Depending on the seller's circumstances and what they are looking for in the sale, different scenarios may appeal to them. Perhaps they are changing jobs and moving cities, in which case they may prefer a quick sale and be more price-flexible. Or they may want or need to stand firm on price for financial reasons and, therefore, may accept a longer closing, which could benefit the investor.

When writing offers as an investor, you can demonstrate this buying power by including a letter showing not just that you are flexible in terms of timing or other conditions, but also that you are a solid buyer who is pre-approved for financing. These might be key factors that appeal to the sellers, and may give you an edge over someone buying the property as a primary home, whose offer may be more limiting than yours, with conditions on financing, a specific closing, or other inclusions.

The bottom line is that investors—especially experienced investors with a savvy agent and team behind them—can creatively structure an offer in a way that gives them a competitive advantage over someone purchasing the property as a primary residence.

(Samples of clauses from different offer letters are included in Appendix C at the back of this book, as well as online at www.realestaterichesbook.com.)

Most purchase and sale agreements come in standard formats with standard clauses and are readily available to your realtor—for example, in Ontario, through the Ontario Real Estate Association (OREA). You then use schedules and custom clauses to expand on what the standard contract deals with or calls for, since most agreements will not be comprehensive enough for your needs. For example, you can ask the sellers of a property to provide a Seller Property Information Statement (SPIS), which they are then obligated to do. Of course, the sellers can reject or amend any schedule or clause, or any part of a contract.

There are many common clauses contained in the purchase and sale agreement, and they cover a variety of circumstances—for example, purchase of a condominium as well as purchase of an income-producing triplex. Depending on your situation, you can pick and choose which clauses are necessary.

Note: Never put a fixed date in these clauses. Instead, put a realistic number of days you will need to get the conditions fulfilled and work done.

THE OFFER PROCESS

Once you have found a property you want to put an offer in on, here is how the typical process unfolds:

1. Your agent writes and submits the offer.

2. The seller often comes back with a counter-offer.

3. You accept the seller's counter-offer or you counter back.

4. Once the offer is accepted, any conditions on the offer need to be fulfilled.

5. Send the offer with the listing to your mortgage broker.

6. Send the offer with the listing to your lawyer.

7. After the conditions are fulfilled, they are removed, and the deal becomes firm.

8. You and the seller proceed to the closing date.

NEGOTIATING TIPS

An experienced real estate agent often proves their mettle—and their value as an asset to your team—when it comes time to negotiate.

Understanding the art and science of negotiating will be important for you as an investor if you want to make money buying and selling real estate. Whether you are a first-time or an experienced investor, you will benefit from the practical tips and street-smart strategies that build negotiating skills.

On almost a daily basis, we all negotiate—whether we are selling, persuading, convincing, or influencing another person's thinking to align with an associate's or our own wants and needs in business, or with our partners or children at home.

Understanding the motivations of all parties to an agreement and using psychological negotiating techniques and concepts will not only give you an edge in real estate investing but also help you save or earn money and win friends and respect in the long run. In real estate negotiations, it's most important to understand why a property is for sale and why a buyer is buying. Being authentic and honest with all parties will make for smoother communications and, potentially, a great agreement at the end.

Before You Make an Offer

There are many steps before making an offer—and this holds true even if you're working with a buyer's realtor.

1. **Determine the price at which the property stops cash flowing:** Before you enter your negotiating process, figure out the maximum price you can pay and still generate a positive cash flow. Doing your homework will put you in a position of strength and confidence from the start, even if you are competing with other buyers. And if you don't end up getting the property, you won't feel badly. It's business.

2. **Remember that you have other options:** Don't think this is the only property you can buy or the only great deal out there. When negotiating, I always find another comparable property. In fact, when making an offer, including an active listing as well as a recently sold comparable in the area will give you credibility; it illustrates you know what is happening in the market. It indicates you are a fair buyer who is not trying to take advantage of a seller's situation (more on this later in the chapter). It also helps the seller's realtor in getting the owner to say yes to the deal—and of course the seller's realtor will appreciate that.

3. **Never get emotionally involved in the property:** By this point in the book, you hopefully understand the difference between buying real estate as an investment and buying a home to live in. This is business, and you must be objective, know your numbers, and offer what makes sense when assessing any potential deal.

As an investor, you're not emotionally attached to the houses you're buying; it's all about being fair and making business sense in any situation. For example, if the home inspection reveals a leaky roof, you can renegotiate the deal before waiving conditions—even if it's discovered after you've made an offer. The new offer can stipulate that either repairs will be made prior to closing or the purchase price will be lowered to reflect the defect. For someone buying the home as a primary residence—your potential competition—finding such a flaw in the property might send them running. But for investors with a little experience and a savvy agent and other strong team members, you could see this as an opportunity to work the challenge to your advantage.

Conversely, precisely because investors aren't emotionally attached to properties, if you discover something about the property you don't like, to the point that it's a "deal breaker," you can easily walk away. A primary home buyer, on the other hand, may be so in love with the house that they overlook or accept flaws and the costs to repair them.

4. **When you work with an area expert, they can negotiate from a place of confidence:** Knowing the area and neighbourhood, and what neighbouring houses have sold for, means that you can be forthright. This is where the power comes in, by choosing the right realtor. This actually is my favourite part of my work—making the deal work for all parties involved.

Understanding why a property is for sale is critical, since this gives you and your realtor leverage when negotiating. There are many reasons a property may be for sale, and each provides clues to how your opposition may think and what you can do to get yourself a good deal as well as help them in the process.

1. Is it a divorce or separation situation?

2. Did one of the owners die?

3. Did someone suffer job loss?

4. Is it job relocation?

5. Does it involve a health issue with one of the owners?

6. Is it retirement?

7. Are the owners downsizing now that the kids are grown? Or upsizing due to a growing family or a promotion?

8. Is the sale prompted by high property taxes?

9. Is it a change in investment strategies of an investor-owner—perhaps they are buying more multi-family investments?

10. Have they found another attractive investment and want to adjust their portfolio to maximize profits?

11. Does one of the owners need to sell due to losses in other investments?

12. Is it a dispute between partners?

13. Is it a seller's market and do the owners believe this is the time to sell and take their profits?

14. Is an owner testing the market?

15. Based on news reports, does the seller believe that a downturn is coming and the time to sell is now?

I can go on and on, but let's take a look at an example from this list.

Buying a property from a couple going through a divorce is not an easy deal to execute. One of them could want to sell high to be stubborn or because they need the money, and the other might want to sell low just to upset their soon-to-be-former spouse.

The urgency is high, since both want to get on with life, but they both may also play hardball in the negotiation. The most important thing to remember is that this is a hard time for them and you are to bring calmness and stability to a tense and strenuous situation. This is the perfect example of where presenting a letter with the offer that summarizes the active and recently sold listings will help tremendously, since it is based on fact and concrete information, not emotions.

Having an informed investor who is ready to buy the property could facilitate a fast sale, which would appeal to the couple because they can then move forward with their lives. It could also benefit the sellers in a different way if there are children involved: for example, an investor could buy the house and allow one of the parents to remain there so the kids can finish the school year. They have the comfort of remaining in the home for some time, while the investor has known tenants who are already living in the property.

The point I want to impress upon you is to take each situation and try to see what's best for all parties. It bothers me so much when I hear investors or buyers ask me to help them buy a property because they know there is a divorce unfolding, and their goal is to squeeze the sellers for every penny because we know they need to sell. I, for one, believe in karma, and I'm not sure how well it bodes for someone's personal or professional success to take such an approach. It's taking advantage of a situation and becoming greedy, plain and simple. Investment real estate is a long-term buy, and in the long run saving a couple thousand dollars is not going to matter as much as making a difference in someone else's life, and working toward a win-win-win situation.

I can't stress enough how important it is to be respectful to all parties when negotiating the offer. It's not about squeezing every last penny from the seller. Be respectful to the seller, the seller's realtor, and your own realtor. I love working with investors because of their open-minded personalities. They communicate what's on their mind, but with respect, to me and all other parties. Yes, we want a great deal, but respect and open communication are very important in each and every deal.

Preparing the Offer

After understanding the motive of the seller, you and your buyer's agent can begin preparing the offer, understanding that negotiation is about the price, but that's only a starting point. Other key elements include:

1. **Closing date:** This is a powerful negotiating tool. Knowing the closing date the seller wants can influence the negotiations in a major way. Unlike a primary home buyer who may need to be in the house by a certain date, such as when school starts, an investor can use the seller's preferred date as leverage in the offer. Make sure you state your flexibility in the letter your realtor presents to the sellers on your behalf.

Note: By law, realtors must present what you say, even if it's an unreasonable offer. The seller, of course, can always say no.

2. **Financing terms:** Working with savvy realtors can make a big difference in facilitating a deal. For example, if one of my clients is retiring and doesn't need money from the sale of the property right away, it's a great opportunity to provide seller's financing, which means my client could defer capital gains taxes. Offer the seller a reasonable rate of return on the money and the investor a way to leverage their capital and credit, and you create a win-win situation for all parties.

3. **Conditions:** Include as many conditions as possible at the outset and lift some, as you need to, while negotiating. Always include a condition that the property pass an inspection, because if an unforeseen problem shows up, you can use this as leverage when negotiating the price.

Remember—be fair to all parties and always think win-win, and you will!

NEGOTIATING DOESN'T END ONCE YOU SUBMIT AN OFFER

My investor-client Steven was looking at putting an offer in on a semi-detached house. The owners were asking $197,000, and we were thinking of offering $193,000 to $195,000, believing that was fair. Steven would then spend about $10,000 on renovations to bring the value to $205,000 to $207,000, in line with other properties on the market.

When we were negotiating price, Steven and his wife were in the car with me, seeing how I negotiate. At all times, I am respectful to all parties, never trying to take advantage of anyone—really just trying to get a fair price for my client. That's my job.

The sellers were in a very bad financial situation. They were actually separating—something their agent should never have told me, because now I was able to use that information to my client's benefit.

Even though we thought getting the property for $195,000 would be good and $193,000 even better, they were adamant they wanted their full $197,000 asking price. "Take it or leave it" was basically their position. Steven and his wife ended up offering the $197,000—which was $2,000 more than what they wanted to pay, but they knew they were going to buy and hold, and they were confident they could get that money back over the long term.

Note: When negotiating a purchase price, don't get too hung up over $1,000 or $2,000, or a similar small amount, letting it become a deal breaker. Over the long term, it will not make a big difference. If you're always rigid and never willing to bend, how wise is that, really? I understand investors want good deals, but at the same time, don't let a relatively small amount of money stop you from getting a good deal on a property that would appreciate more than average.

So, Steven and his wife met the couple's demands for $197,000. During the inspection, however, some unexpected flaws were revealed. We went back to the seller's agent and explained the issues found in the inspection, and said that we wanted to be fair with the approximately $5,000 repair costs. We initially suggested splitting the difference, but because the seller wanted to close the sale more quickly, they absorbed more of the repair cost and we ended up getting the property for $192,500—less than the $193,000 Steven was initially aiming for as the best-case scenario.

The lesson here is that the negotiation isn't over once you submit an offer; it can continue through the inspection. In the inspection clause, you can specify what will happen if flaws are revealed: you could agree, for example, that the seller pays for the repairs and the deal closes, or that the buyer doesn't want the property and walks away, or that you split the cost 50/50, or that the seller reduces the asking price by the cost of the repairs.

There are also options in the offer for the negotiation to be reopened (after the offer has been accepted) if issues are found during inspection.

For examples of clauses and conditions, see Appendix C.

13

After the Purchase

If you thought the hard work you put into planning, researching, and negotiating to buy investment property was all you had to do, think again. Once you've bought the property, you become a landlord and must do what you can to maximize the profits in your business.

HOW TO INCREASE CASH FLOW

As we discussed earlier, for a real estate investor using the buy and hold strategy, cash flow is king. And cash flow is largely determined by your basic financial picture: how much money you have for a down payment, the purchase price of the property and how much of that you have to borrow in the form of a mortgage, and how much rent you are able to charge, given the type of property and the area in which it is located.

Your cash flow *must* be positive. The monthly rent you charge has to exceed the amount of your mortgage payment and expenses combined. Your expenses include everything to do with running your business, such as taxes, management fees, advertising costs, bank fees, and maintenance and repair services. Be sure to calculate these on a monthly basis, even if they are paid annually (for example, property taxes) in order to get an accurate picture of your monthly cash flow.

Obviously, the more you are able to collect in rent—but, importantly, without pricing yourself out of the market—and the better you can control your expenses, the more positive cash flow you can generate.

Since your expenses are a relatively fixed and constant part of your business, the trick is to find innovative ways to increase your cash flow by generating more revenue. Some of these involve modifications at the time you buy and prepare your investment property for market, such as upgrades to appliances and fixtures, and other cosmetic improvements such as painting, adding new floors, door handles, or basic landscaping. These improvements will allow you to charge a premium on the monthly rent, compared to competing properties, which may have lower quality or fewer standard items.

Still, it is important to not overspend; don't make so many improvements (or unnecessary ones) that you have to charge a huge premium on the average rent for your area just to offset your renovation costs. (See the Top 5 Tips below for ideas on how to get the most bang for your buck.)

Other tricks for generating more revenue involve ongoing management techniques, such as levying fees to process tenant applications or late rent payments, adding a charge for pets or additional parking, and renting out storage space. Before implementing any of these techniques, you should always check the provincial and municipal tenant legislation to make sure there are no restrictions against such actions.

TAHANI'S TOP 5 TIPS TO INCREASE CASH FLOW

1. **Painting:** Dollar for dollar, painting your investment property before you first rent it out has the greatest return on investment. Spending a few hundred dollars to revitalize key interior areas creates the impression that the property is clean, fresh, and newly renovated. Not only does this allow you to potentially charge more rent, but the side benefit is that it may encourage your tenants to maintain the property better to keep it looking clean and bright.

2. **Appliances and fixtures:** Upgrading the quality of appliances and of kitchen and bathroom fixtures will lend a premium feel to the unit, which is conducive to charging a higher rent. These days, given the popularity of home improvement stores, there is a vast array of such items at very reasonable prices. For larger appliances, you may be able to get better deals at shopping clubs and

discount outlets, or by looking for "scratch and dent" items that retailers cannot sell at full price. Quite often, these flaws are only cosmetic, and you may be able to fix them yourself. Depending on the placement of the appliance within the property, and as long as the defects don't affect the item's operation, your tenant may not even notice.

3. **Parking:** Parking spaces are another excellent way to generate more revenue. You could charge a premium for a space, on top of the monthly rent for the property itself. If you have a garage or carport, you may be able to charge an additional premium for "covered" or "indoor" parking. And if you have any parking spaces not allocated to tenants, consider renting those out to neighbouring residents or business people. For example, some owners of downtown condo units rent out their parking spaces to someone other than the tenant who lives in their unit, such as workers from nearby office towers. In such cases, however, you should always check with the condominium corporation to make sure you're allowed to do this.

4. **Lighting:** Upgrading the light fixtures and type of lighting (such as energy-efficient bulbs) produces multiple benefits. Again, it creates the feeling that the property is modern and up to date. It also affords a well-lit, safe, and comfortable environment, and any energy-efficiency gains will no doubt be appreciated by your tenant, assuming they're the ones paying the utilities. Like appliances and fixtures, lighting systems are relatively low-cost items that yield high return on investment.

5. **Flooring:** There are so many economical and durable flooring options on the market today that making any necessary flooring replacements or repairs can easily be cost-effective. Like freshly painted walls, clean, fresh, and modern flooring really helps set the tone of the property, and could go a long way in how your tenant perceives and maintains the property. For example, if your tenant demographic is professionals, don't expect that old beat-up linoleum flooring will cut it for them.

Additional improvements you can make to the property to maximize its appeal to tenants include:

- Clean the carpets and walls, and repair any damage.

- Install new doorknobs and kitchen-cupboard handles; they help make a good first impression that everything is modern and functional.

- Replace the countertops; they don't have to be expensive granite, just something up to date and new.

- Replace bathroom fixtures such as shower heads and faucets; they can give a feeling of "new and expensive" but be purchased very economically.

- Do some landscaping in the front yard; even a few hundred dollars can boost first-impression curb appeal and make buyers think the inside of a property will be just as nice.

- Consider painting the kitchen cupboards instead of installing new ones.

- Change the front door; for a few hundred dollars, it can have a huge impact on curb appeal and the overall impression.

- Add a patio or a deck; these projects are a little more expensive, but add tremendous value—if you don't get too carried away with the design.

MANAGING YOUR PROPERTY

Now that you've bought your investment property and have made some improvements to increase its appeal, you'll need to turn your attention to getting it rented. This is something you can do yourself, although many investors turn to the professionals for help. Some realtors who may not be busy selling homes or who may be doing their clients the odd favour do help match rental properties with tenants; you may even occasionally see "For Rent" listings on the MLS®. However, renting and managing property are very different activities from what a realtor does, particularly one like me who specializes in dealing with investors. Renting and managing property are best left to a property manager, not a realtor—or at least not the investor-savvy agent you're looking for. They should be focused on their specialty.

Note: There is a difference between a jack-of-all-trades and a specialist. Find a realtor who only buys and sells real estate, and a property manager who only manages property.

When I work with investors, I always ask them what they prefer to do in terms of property management. There are three main options:

- Rent the property yourself. Many novice investors are inclined to go the do-it-yourself route, both for the learning experience and to save property management fees. But I always caution that, just like anything else, this takes time, effort, and often money. After all, if you're managing your own property, who are your tenants going to call when a pipe bursts or the furnace breaks down at 3 a.m. in the middle of winter? You!

- Hire a property manager and be very involved in the process until you learn and understand enough to be able to manage a property on your own.

- Hire a property manager, oversee them as necessary, and move on to find the next investment. This is the most popular choice for seasoned investors. You never totally walk away, but you find a good property manager and trust them, while still managing them like you would any other "employee" in your company. As CEO, make sure you stay on top of your investment at all times, and make sure your property manager provides regular general and expense reports, which you should look over closely.

As a real estate investor, finding a quality property manager will be one of the more challenging parts of building your team. They are worth their weight in gold. Find a good one in your area and hang on to them, for they will prove their value over and over. Always keep in touch and try to strengthen the relationship. When looking for a property manager, go the same route you did for an investor-savvy realtor:

- Get referrals from fellow investors.

- Interview at least two or three prospective candidates.

- Ask about their experience and the types of tenants they usually deal with.

- Make sure they understand the market you're buying in, the tenant profile, and how much rent you can get for your property.

When I show properties to clients, we can see that some areas attract a higher-end tenant profile. Some starter tenants, such as a young couple just starting life together, want a rental that is appropriate for their stage in life—a place to call home that's not too expensive. A savvy property manager understands that different areas attract different types of tenants, and they understand which one you're after and how to market the property to attract that type of tenant.

Note: Higher-end tenants aren't necessarily a guarantee that the property will be better cared for than if rented to starter tenants.

Setting the appropriate rent is important. If you can get a good, reliable tenant renting for $1,250 per month, but you price the property too high, say at $1,300, you risk having it sit vacant. Trying to gain an extra $50 per month (which is only $600 per year) could wind up costing you $1,300 *per month* for every month it sits empty. It's better to attract and keep a good tenant over time than to run the risk of the property not generating revenue for any length of time.

TAHANI'S TIP

When buying a property as an investor, try to close mid-month. This gives you a couple of weeks to go in and paint or do other minor improvements before you rent it out for the beginning of the next month. This eliminates the property from being vacant for any length of time.

Just as realtors specialize in different types of markets, so, too, do property managers. For example, some property managers lease only fully furnished units to executives of large employers in an area. Find one who specializes in the type of property you own.

Property managers also provide a range of services, and you can pick and choose to fit your strategy. You can ask them to lease (find a tenant for) the property for you, and leave it at that; or you can get them to lease as well as manage the property on a month-to-month basis. Or you can lease the property yourself and get them to manage it for you. With any of these choices, you still should visit your tenants at least twice a year and always keep the lines of communication open. Smart investors look upon their tenants as "partners" in their business, even if their primary point of contact is a property manager. And it is an important relationship for you to manage.

Most property managers write advertisements for rental properties, but I advise clients to always—*always*—write their own ads. Why? There is no one who knows the property better—you understand the economic fundamentals of the area, the amenities, the type of tenant you want to attract, and the specific features of the house. At the very least, you should write your ads in co-operation with the property manager.

Your realtor and property manager should also know where to place the ad for best results. In Kitchener-Waterloo and Cambridge, for example, Kijiji is the number one website for finding tenants. In Toronto or Vancouver, it might be craigslist. Find out which is the most effective website in your area and advertise there.

Note: At all times, investors should be managing their property managers—you should always know what your property manager is doing on your behalf, and how and when they are doing it.

CASE STUDY: LAURA LEARNS THE HARD WAY

Here's a good example to illustrate my point about managing your property manager. I sold a house that I knew could rent for $1,350 to an investor named Laura. We decided on a property manager, and I advised her to keep active with the property manager. She was a first-time investor and rather inexperienced.

Laura paid the property manager an upfront fee to look for a tenant for her house. After a month, she still didn't have a tenant. I asked if she called the property manager for updates on when and how many times the property was shown, and what the typical feedback was from prospective renters. She relayed to me that the property manager told her the market wasn't good and the area wasn't good enough to attract $1,350—in February, but that things should improve in March.

I stressed to her to get direct answers from the property manager about where the house was being advertised, when it was being shown, and what the specific feedback was—from the manager as well as from prospective tenants who viewed it.

After two and a half months went by, and still nothing happened, she called me, stressed out and not sure what to do. I encouraged her to call in another property manager, ask for suggestions on the amount of rent to charge, how long it would take to rent—and all the other pertinent questions. Laura took it from there. My goal was to teach and educate her rather than do all the work for her. She saw the benefits of hiring a different property manager, even though she was worried about losing the fee she'd paid, and about what the first property manager would think of her.

Laura finally summoned the courage to call the first property manager to cancel that arrangement. She never got her retainer refunded, but at this point all she wanted to do was move on. She contracted the second property manager and, learning from her first experience, was clearer in her expectations about being kept informed when the property was shown, to whom, and what the feedback was.

After four showings in two and a half weeks, the new property manager rented the house, for the full $1,350 rental rate! Laura called, excited and happy about renting the house—after learning a pretty important lesson the hard way.

Laura's example shows you how important it is to stay on top of not just your property manager and realtor but also your entire team—to not just rely on them and assume they are working for you, but to take an active role to ensure they are doing what they're supposed to do.

CASE STUDY: PETER TAKES *TOO MUCH* CONTROL FROM THE START

Another example is Peter, an investor-client of mine who bought a property in a very nice, active area.

Since the house was in an area that had a lot of traffic—though not too much—I advised Peter that all he really had to do was put a "For Rent" sign out front and it would draw attention. As a first-time investor, he was keen to rent the place himself so he could learn as much as he could about being a landlord and dealing with tenants directly.

We estimated the property could rent for $1,250 to $1,295 per month. After many showings—several per week—Peter still hadn't rented it, so he dropped the rent from $1,295 to $1,200, and even that price, he said, was not working.

I knew other investors in the area who got $1,295 to $1,325 for similar properties. I wanted to figure out why his property hadn't rented yet, so I asked Peter what he was doing when he showed the property. He explained that he wasn't doing anything out of the ordinary, just doing his job and showing prospective tenants around the house.

I was intrigued, so the following week I accompanied Peter on some showings to observe what he was, or was not, doing. It was obvious that Peter was making a fairly typical rookie mistake: he was all over the people as they toured the unit. He followed them closely from room to room, breathing down their necks, not allowing them any free roaming time, and he constantly asked what it would take for them to "do a deal" with him. He sounded desperate. He didn't ask about what they were looking for, their interests, their needs, or anything like that.

Imagine how those people must have felt. Perhaps there was something wrong with the place or some other reason for Peter's desperation to rent it? Not a good sign. They also must have worried that he would similarly breathe down their necks as a landlord if they chose to move in.

After everyone left, I explained what he was doing and how with subtle changes he could make a deal with the tenants. I encouraged him to worry less about renting the property and think more about understanding the tenants and their needs. Understanding that the landlord-tenant relationship is very important, were they a match for him and his property? Why try to rent it to someone who is not excited about the place and living there? We went over such details as well as how he should talk less and listen more. (By the way, Peter's mistake is one a lot of realtors make when showing properties for sale.) We decided to set up another open house, and I would be present to observe.

Right away I noticed how Peter introduced himself and presented each visitor with an information sheet, and then encouraged them to look around on their own, saying he'd be happy to speak with them when they were finished their tour. He simply stood back and let them view the property on their own, at their own pace. As they were leaving, he asked some basic questions in a friendly manner: what they liked about the place, what they didn't like, where they were renting now, and so on—questions to produce feedback and information that would be helpful. For example, if the prospective tenants said they were presently paying $750, then his house would be a big jump for them. These questions helped Peter qualify the tenants, to see if they would be a good fit—he wanted to find a great tenant, not just any tenant out of desperation.

The next week, Peter did three showings using his new approach, and he chose to rent to a couple for $1,250 per month. He believed he could have gotten more, but he liked the couple and what they had to say about the property. He thought that they would be good tenants. Peter's instincts were right: they've now been there a year and a half with no issues, and have been perfect tenants for Peter as a first-time investor.

CASE STUDY: ALICIA DOESN'T TAKE *ENOUGH* CONTROL

Alicia, a novice investor, bought a semi-detached home from me in 2007. It was in a nice area, showed beautifully, and was easy to tenant. After just a few years of owning the property, Alicia called me in frustration, wanting to sell the property because she was having a lot of trouble with the property manager, who didn't return phone calls or communicate with her at all. I listened to Alicia complain about the property manager. I then asked her about how often she called the property manager. Had she ever visited her tenants? Did she even know their phone number? To my surprise, Alicia hadn't visited the house for two and a half years!

Can you imagine deciding to become an investor, with all kinds of hopes and plans to become successful, and spending all that money to buy a place—and to be so turned off by your experience with your property manager that you don't even visit the house or your tenants for two and a half years? It was almost as if Alicia had resigned herself to the fact that this was how real estate investing was done, and she essentially let go of her own investment and goals.

She blamed the property manager and the tenants and many other things, but did not take responsibility for not being there or taking control of the situation. If one property manager isn't working out, find another one. Take an active role.

While her response was far from acceptable—or necessary—it certainly was understandable. It's an excellent example of investors who think real estate is a passive investment, as well as a reminder of how important it is to take your time and choose your team members wisely. This is exactly how they can affect a relationship and your investment performance.

Note: Visit your tenants at least twice a year. Not only does it make good business sense, it shows them that you care about your property and about them.

14 Setting Goals

I have found that there are basically two types of investors. Some are very ambitious and have plans to buy a certain number of properties in a specific time frame. They have a clear vision of what they want (though it's not always realistic); they just lack the experience and know-how to get there. Other investors suffer from "paralysis by analysis"—they want to invest in real estate, but are so unsure of how and where and when to start that they take seminar after seminar and read book after book. For these would-be investors, the determining factor that keeps them on the sidelines is fear—they are afraid of taking that important first step.

If you are a novice investor, you do want to take it slow: look carefully for your first investment, learn the ropes, make sure you really understand and are comfortable with everything, buy a property that fits your strategy, find a good tenant, operate your property well and profitably—and then move on to your next investment.

Indeed, you *need* to take it one step at a time. Becoming a sophisticated real estate investor is a process, not a one-time event. Nor is it a get-rich-quick scheme, no matter what those popular TV shows may tell you. The buy and hold strategy requires a long-term commitment—a minimum of five to seven years for each property you own. With such a timeline, if you base your decisions on fundamentals and solid research, and truly understand the areas you're investing in and the rental demographics for your neighbourhoods, chances are your investment will do well over the long term. You—or rather, your tenants—will have paid down your mortgage, you will have benefitted from the positive monthly cash flow, and the value of your property will likely have increased.

Mind you, there will always be risk; no investment, not even real estate, is risk free. But the objective is to take *calculated* risks, to turn the *possibility* of success into the *probability* of success. Setting goals and planning properly will help maximize the probability of success.

YOUR "PERSONAL BELIZE"

Don Campbell, president of the Real Estate Investment Network (REIN), always asks new members to envision their ultimate goal—their "personal Belize," as he calls it. Is it to retire? Build a nest egg for your kids' educations? Take care of your grandchildren? What is *your* ultimate goal? Why are you investing and what do you hope to achieve?

These are key questions I always ask prospective clients very early in the process. Experienced investors typically answer that they see themselves on a beach with a computer, reviewing their investments from a distance while they relax and enjoy their success. For others, it might be to save for their kids' educations or to donate money and time to a cause they believe in. Each person has different reasons.

Many novice investors are looking to augment or replace the income from their regular day jobs. They think: there has to be a better way than working, working, working, right? Or they're working on a retirement plan or an education plan and they want an investment property that will help to fund their retirement or tuition expenses.

When I meet with new clients, I ask them to describe their vision of where they're going, their goals and timelines. Then we map out a plan to start them on the road to getting there. For example, if they're buying a house to save for their kids' educations and the kids are four or five years old, that basically gives us 12 to 15 years to work with. If someone says they want to make $1 million in five years, I might offer a little more realistic viewpoint. I don't want to tell them it can't be done, but I caution them against being too ambitious and focusing too much on the end goal and not enough on all the work and proper steps it takes to get there.

If a client says they want to find an investment property that will yield $200 to $300 in monthly cash flow, that's actually very reasonable and we can quite realistically devise a plan to make that happen. To do this, of course, we must remember to factor in all costs, such as property management fees, vacancy costs, taxes, and other items that can eat into monthly cash flow. Novice investors often overlook these when crunching the numbers on prospective properties.

For example, let's say the investors, Jill and Tony, have children who are still very young, giving us 12 to 15 years to achieve their goals. A sensible plan would be to buy two or three properties using a buy and hold strategy. A key objective of this strategy—a must, actually—is that the properties generate positive cash flow immediately. Jill and Tony are not really savvy investors; they want something easy, low maintenance, and less hands-on, so we might start by looking at semi-detached homes, townhouses, and maybe even condominiums, and we would look at good areas that attract good tenants with less turnover.

Jim, on the other hand, has different goals and is looking at this more as a business; he may even consider doing it full-time if all goes well. With Jim, we could look at the same types of properties as with Jill and Tony, but we can also get him into older properties that may need a little work such as painting, changing light fixtures, and improving the flooring.

For Jill and Tony, I would do more of the work and help them find places that fit their model. I would be very careful to explain why I advise certain properties or areas, taking care to make sure they understood everything that was happening.

I would also educate Jim, but I would expect him to do a little more of the research himself, because it's important that he learn, not just follow my lead. I want him to know what makes one area or property better than another, so he is able to make such judgments on his own.

A good analogy would be that with Jill and Tony, we're all going fishing together and I am fishing along with them, helping them understand the concepts and techniques involved in fishing, but not expecting them to become fishermen—or fisherwomen—on their own. With Jim, I'm teaching him how to fish, with the intent that he will be a self-sufficient fisherman as quickly as possible. As real estate investors, Jill and Tony aren't as serious about building their portfolio quickly. Jim's plans are more aggressive, so he needs to understand everything himself.

BEING WEALTHY VERSUS RICH

As you set your goals, keep in mind that becoming a successful sophisticated real estate investor is more about being "wealthy" than being "rich." You might not realize the difference, but it is quite significant. Being wealthy is all about lifestyle, balance, and giving. Being rich, on the other hand, is about making money, period. You become so focused on getting rich that you forget about living your life. Lots of people are very successful in the financial sense, but they are so consumed by their work that their business becomes their life.

I, too, for a time was focused on getting rich, guilty of not living in balance. Given my upbringing and background, for much of my life all I wanted to do was "make it,"—to survive and to provide well for my children. In doing that, I forgot about myself, my friends, my life. I was focused only on work, work, work, and I didn't enjoy and celebrate the small successes and big moments and other important steps along the way. Once I realized the difference, I started enjoying some of life's simplest pleasures, such as learning to swim and to ride a bike—two activities I mastered only very recently.

Live SIMPLE

SIMPLE—Significantly Impacting Many People's Lives Every day.

Some people are intent on making a big difference in the world by doing big things. But it's not always about making a big impact; sometimes it's the little things that make a huge difference, such as making the waitress at the restaurant you're eating in feel special. Practise random acts of kindness, even in little ways, such as sitting and talking with someone. That can be huge in someone's life. People sometimes tell me I inspire them. I don't necessarily set out to inspire them, I just listen carefully so I understand exactly what it is they want, and then I use that information and approach in dealing with them. They often are left feeling, "Wow, there is someone who is truly listening."

Attitude of Gratitude

Another technique I use is to try to live with an "attitude of gratitude." Every day, I make it a point to reach out to people, to send a thank-you note or a small gift to a client, contact, referral, or even a tenant. I literally do this every day. I have a large contact list, and there is always someone who deserves a "thank you." I love doing it because it makes me feel great, but more importantly, small gestures can make a big difference in someone's day, simply by showing you appreciate them.

So, as you map out your real estate career and build your network of team members and contacts, keep things in perspective and consider showing your gratitude along the way.

MAPPING OUT A PLAN

Once you have given some thought to your long-term goals, you'll need to consider how to achieve them. This is something I explore all the time with new clients when we meet. They typically ask: Where do I start? What is the best strategy for me? Where do I make the most money, and how do I do that? Clients always want the easiest, fastest, best, and most profitable way to get to where they want to go. This is where your investor-savvy agent can help by mapping out a plan to get you there.

Here's another way of looking at it: Let's say you have decided you want to go to New York City. You've heard it's a great city to visit, with a lot of fun things to see and do. The first question on your mind is likely: What's the best way to get there? It's a great question, but it happens to be the *wrong* question. The right question is: Where am I now? Only when you know where you are, can you determine how to get to your destination.

The same is true in real estate investing. If you're a first-time investor, you have to figure out where you are now before you can figure out where you're going. For example, if you have $50,000 for a down payment, that's very different from having $250,000. And that's very different from having no money to put down. In each of these scenarios, the starting point—the down payment—is a key determinant in mapping out your destination in terms of the type of property you can buy, the cost, and how large a role this property can play in helping you achieve your goals. Another important factor to consider is your knowledge and experience. Is this your first real estate investment or your fourth?

So, using the New York City example again, how far is it from where you are? Knowing that, how will you get to your destination, what are your options? Do you want to drive, fly, cycle, or take a bus or boat? There are many ways to get there, but costs and trip durations vary. Let's say your starting point is Toronto. You can fly—it gets you there quickly, but it costs a lot. You can drive—it costs less but it takes longer. Your journey could be smooth or you could face challenges. If you're flying, the flight might be delayed, or bad weather could cause you to land in another city. If you're driving, your car could overheat, the battery could die, or you may need to detour to avoid construction.

You may face similar challenges on your real estate journey. For example, you may run into problems with your property manager and have to fire him or her. Or, despite your best efforts, your tenants may not turn out to be perfect and you have to evict them. Or your plans to install new roofing on a property may be hit with higher labour costs and material shortages.

In planning toward your long-term goals, once you've decided on how best to get there, you need to think about short-term questions. Consider visiting New York as your long-term goal and taking the plane is your strategy for getting there. Now you need to ask short-term questions such as where to buy your plane ticket, when to depart and return, what you can afford to spend, which hotel to stay at, and which sights to see during the time you're there.

In the same way, you will face short-term questions when investing in real estate. What area should I buy in? What type of property? When do I meet with a mortgage broker? And so on. As you can see, it takes planning, time, and effort to know where you are and where you're heading.

Exit Strategies

In real estate investing, having an exit strategy simply means having a plan for how and, approximately, when you want to divest yourself of a property. It could be that your research has determined the economic growth for an area has peaked and it might be a good time to sell, or that you want to buy in another area poised for strong growth.

It sounds simple enough, but novice investors often overlook having clearly defined exit strategies—notice that I'm suggesting you have more than one—in place for each property. Let's say you bought a property using the buy and hold strategy and plan to sell it after 10 years. What happens if the market is down when it comes time to sell? You would be wise to have an alternative strategy so you can avoid potentially selling it at an undervalued price. You could, for example, enter into a lease- or rent-to-own arrangement with a long-term tenant who is ready to buy, you could take on a joint venture partner, or you could renovate and sell the property in order to command a higher price. Or, as long as the property was still cash-flowing, you could continue to rent it out and sell it once the market recovers.

SAMPLE EXIT STRATEGIES

Lease- or rent-to-own: Leasing or renting the property to a tenant who will become the owner, with part of their monthly rent going toward their down payment

Refinance: Could involve refinancing an existing mortgage, taking on a joint venture partner, or offering financing such as a vendor take-back mortgage

Sale of property: Outright sale of property and title to another party, be it an investor or primary home buyer

Flip: Renovating the property to command a higher price, and selling it—not as risky as a straight fix and flip, since the investor has owned the property for a number of years and has already gained from the value appreciation, mortgage paydown, and positive cash flow

Your investor-savvy agent can help you devise suitable exit strategies that fit your system and plan. And the time to do this is when you buy, not years down the road when, heaven forbid, you *need* to sell for some reason. Mapping out potential exit strategies at the beginning of, and throughout, your real estate investing journey will keep you in a position of strength, so if your research indicates you should be thinking about selling in year five, then you are prepared and can position yourself to get fair value for the property. If you don't have an exit strategy, then market conditions, rising interest rates, the performance of the property, or other factors could dictate the outcome for you.

For example, imagine you own a property with a joint venture partner, and that partner is going through a divorce or illness and wants to sell the property. If you haven't considered such a contingency in your exit strategy, you could find yourself at his or her mercy and be forced to sell or find another partner. Having to sell quickly or unexpectedly may mean you have to price the property accordingly, potentially losing thousands of dollars, cutting into your profits, and causing aggravation and headaches.

Know your exit strategy ahead of time. Do not wait until something happens and your hand is forced. Plan at least two exit strategies for each property before you need to sell.

TAHANI'S TIPS

- Think long term in your investment strategy.

- Establish your goals.

- Develop at least two exit strategies for each property.

- Plan *practically* for the future, so you don't end up looking *wishfully* at the past.

- Aim to be "wealthy" versus "rich."

- Live SIMPLE.

15

Conclusion: Your Future

In thinking about the principles and strategies presented in this book, you are taking your first steps toward becoming a knowledgeable real estate investor. You have a better idea of the questions to ask of your team of experts, and hopefully a map to follow.

But before you turn the final pages, close the cover of this book, and get to work taking control of your financial future, let's review some key points that underline certain messages I want to leave with you. These will serve as good starting points for you as you begin your journey. From time to time, revisit them to remind yourself why you want to invest in real estate and how you're going to achieve your goals.

Your "Big Why": Why do you want to invest in real estate? Is it to build your retirement nest egg, to pay for your kids' post-secondary education, or to become a full-time investor? Whatever your "why" is, make sure you choose the right strategy to get you there. And find an investor-savvy agent who can help you achieve your goals. They understand investment real estate, are very knowledgeable about local market fundamentals, and know how to identify strong potential markets and properties. Find other investors with experience in the strategy you're going to use, and nurture your relationships with them.

Run your business with a clear plan: When you're clear about your "Big Why," your goals, and what you're doing, the "how" becomes easier to find. If your goals are unrealistic, change them as necessary. Don't get stuck with unrealistic objectives that will only produce frustration. At the same time, you shouldn't change your goals too frequently. It's difficult to hit a moving target. You want to strike a good balance between having reasonable, achievable objectives and setting goals that will force you to get outside your comfort zone.

Clarify your goals and objectives by writing them down—then revisit them once a month until they become reality. Something magical happens when you commit to your goals on paper. They begin to take root. When you focus on them repeatedly, you nurture them and they begin to grow. It's important to be clear about your purpose, goals, and strategies. Begin by asking yourself the following questions:

- What strategy am I pursuing?

- What will I do with the properties I buy?

- How many deals per year will I do?

- How much profit will I earn per deal?

- Who can I talk to or connect with to get me closer to my goals?

- What kind of life do I want to live outside of my office/work/job?

- What type of people do I need to surround myself with to succeed?

- How can I lead by example in everything that I do?

- How many lives can I impact by doing this?

You are the CEO of your own business: Always remember that investing in real estate is a business—*your* business—and you are the CEO, no one else. The professionals you work with, your team of experts, also work *for* you and your company, so make sure you make good choices—find people you trust and who will work hard for you, and nurture these important relationships.

Conduct yourself with professionalism and integrity: Make sure strong values are part of your personal calling card—"Do unto others as you would have them do unto you"—and make sure that the way you conduct yourself and your business always reflects these principles. You will gain the respect and admiration of not just your team of advisers but also other people you deal with, and this will stand you well in the long run.

The value of an investor-savvy realtor: One of the most important members of your team is a knowledgeable agent who has experience working with investors and expertise in your target market. Finding such an agent is essential to your success—so when you do find one, pay close attention to maintaining that relationship, and show your appreciation by referring other investors to him or her.

You and your team: Building a strong team of knowledgeable experts— such as your lawyer, broker, accountant, and property manager—is vital, but you also need to maintain that team. You should always be networking and looking for other potential members in case you need them at some point in the future. A new target market or a different property type may demand a new expert, so stay on the lookout for other professionals who can help you.

Take responsibility: There is no reason you can't start now and do well at investing in real estate. Don't blame your situation, your parents, kids, spouse, upbringing, your job, or whatever other excuses you can come up with. Take responsibility now, and take action.

This is only the beginning: Your journey does not end when you finish this book. Now that you have read *Real Estate Riches*, go out and start applying what we have shared here with you. Make your dream a reality.

I was once in your shoes, and I took my interest in real estate and turned it into a successful business. You can, too. I believe in you and what you are capable of accomplishing.

And if you have any questions or need any guidance, once again I invite you to contact me through my website, www.realestaterichesbook.com. Be it in several months or in a couple years, I would love to hear from you, about how you are doing with investing and about how you are well on your way to building your own Real Estate Riches.

Appendix A: Online Resources

Financial Services

    BMO Financial Group – www.bmo.com
    CIBC World Markets – www.cibcwm.com
    Royal Bank of Canada – www.rbc.com
    Scotiabank – www.scotiabank.com
    TD Bank Financial Group – www.td.com

Realty Industry

    Alberta Real Estate Association – www.abrea.ab.ca
    Association of Saskatchewan REALTORS® –
        www.saskatchewanrealestate.com
    British Columbia Real Estate Association – www.bcrea.bc.ca
    The Canadian Real Estate Association – www.crea.ca –
        www.realtor.ca – www.mls.ca
    Fédération des chambres immobilières du Québec – www.fciq.ca
    House Price Index – www.housepriceindex.ca
    Manitoba Real Estate Association – www.realestatemanitoba.com
    New Brunswick Real Estate Association – http://boards.mls.ca/nbrea
    The Newfoundland & Labrador Association of REALTORS® –
        http://boards.mls.ca/nl

Nova Scotia Association of REALTORS® – www.nsar-mls.ca
Ontario Real Estate Association – www.orea.com
Prince Edward Island Real Estate Association –
    www.peirea.com
Real Estate Board of Greater Vancouver – www.rebgv.org
Real Estate Council of Ontario – www.reco.on.ca
Teranet – www.teranet.ca
Toronto Real Estate Board – www.torontorealestateboard.com
Yukon Real Estate Association – www.yrea.ca

Home Building Industry

Building Industry and Land Development Association –
    www.bildgta.ca
Canadian Home Builders' Association – www.chba.ca
Ontario Home Builders' Association – http://ohba.ca

Realtors

Century 21 Canada – www.century21.ca
RE/MAX Canada – www.remax.ca
RE/MAX Fit To Buy – www.fittobuy.ca
Royal LePage – www.royallepage.ca
Sutton Realty – www.sutton.com

Commercial Realtors

Avison Young – www.avisonyoung.com
CB Richard Ellis – www.cbre.com
Colliers International – www.colliersmn.com
Cushman & Wakefield – www.cushwake.com

Research Consultancies

The Conference Board of Canada – www.conferenceboard.ca
Don R. Campbell – www.donrcampbell.com
The Fraser Institute – www.fraserinstitute.org
Urbanation – www.urbanation.ca

Media

CBC – www.cbc.ca
Calgary Herald – www.calgaryherald.com
Canadian Mortgage Trends – www.canadianmortgagetrends.com
Canadian Real Estate magazine – www.canadianrealestatemagazine.ca
The Globe and Mail – www.theglobeandmail.com
homeTRADER – www.hometrader.ca
Investopedia – www.investopedia.com
MoneySense magazine – www.moneysense.ca
National Post – www.nationalpost.com
Ottawa Citizen – www.ottawacitizen.com
Property Wire Canada – www.propertywire.ca
Real Estate News Exchange – www.renx.ca
The Toronto Star – www.thestar.com
The Vancouver Sun – www.vancouversun.com
Winnipeg Free Press – www.winnipegfreepress.com
Your Home – www.yourhome.ca

Professional Services

Appraisal Institute of Canada – www.aicanada.ca
Canadian Association of Accredited Mortgage Professionals –
    www.caamp.org
Canadian Association of Home and Property Inspectors – www.cahpi.ca
The Canadian Bar Association – www.cba.org
The Canadian Institute of Chartered Accountants – www.cica.ca
Canadian Life and Health Insurance Association Inc. – www.clhia.ca
Certified General Accountants Association of Canada –
    www.cga-canada.org
Certified Management Accountants of Canada –
    www.cma-canada.org
Equifax Canada – www.equifax.ca
The Financial Advisors Association of Canada – www.advocis.ca
Financial Planning Standards Council – www.fpsc.ca
Insurance Brokers Association of Canada – www.ibac.ca
TransUnion Canada – www.transunion.ca

Social Media

Facebook – www.facebook.com
LinkedIn – www.linkedin.com
Twitter – http://twitter.com

Investment Groups

Canadian Real Estate Investment Group – www.canreig.com
Professional Real Estate Investors Group – www.preigcanada.com
The Real Estate Investment Network – www.reincanada.com
REIN Research Reports – http://myreinspace.com

Government

Bank of Canada – www.bankofcanada.ca
Canada Mortgage and Housing Corporation – www.cmhc-schl.gc.ca
Canada Revenue Agency – www.cra-arc.gc.ca
Statistics Canada – www.statcan.gc.ca

Appendix B: Glossary

Adjustable mortgage interest rate   A mortgage arrangement whereby both the interest rate and mortgage payment vary, depending on market conditions.

Amortization   The period of time over which a mortgage is to be paid to zero balance, with payments made on a regular basis. Amortization periods are typically 15, 20, 25, or 30 years long. As of March 18, 2011, the Canadian federal government reduced the maximum amortization period to 30 years (from 35) for new government-backed insured mortgages with loan-to-value ratios of more than 80 per cent.

Appraisal   The process of determining the market value of a property.

Appraised value   The estimated value of a property determined by a certified appraiser, usually used for mortgage financing.

Appreciation   The increase in the value of a property over time.

Approved lender   A lending institution authorized by the federal government to make loans under the terms of the National Housing Act. Only approved lenders can negotiate mortgages that require insurance.

Assumption   A legal document signed by a homebuyer that requires the buyer to assume responsibility for the obligations of a mortgage placed on the property by the builder or original owner.

Balanced market   Market conditions when demand for property equals supply. Prices remain stable, leading to reasonable selling periods and offers.

Blended payment   A mortgage payment that includes principal and interest, paid regularly during the term of the mortgage. Payment total remains the same, with the principal portion increasing over time and the interest portion decreasing.

Builder   The company that constructs properties.

Building permit   A certificate that the property owner or contractor must obtain from the municipality before a building can be erected or repaired. It must be posted in a conspicuous place until the job is completed and passed as satisfactory by a municipal building inspector.

Buyer's market   Market conditions when supply of property exceeds demand. Prices may decline, homes may remain on the market longer, and buyers have more leverage.

Canada Mortgage and Housing Corporation (CMHC)   A federal Crown corporation that administers the National Housing Act. CMHC also provides mortgage loan insurance.

Capitalization rate (cap rate)   The ratio between the net operating income of a property and the purchase price or its current market value.

Carriage home   Also known as a link home, where two individual homes are joined by a garage or basement walls so that the houses appear to be single-family homes. They are usually less expensive than fully detached units.

Cash flow   In the context of investment properties, the amount of money left over from the rent payment, after all expenses—such as mortgage, taxes, insurance, maintenance, property management fees, and lawyer and realtor fees—have been paid.

Certificate of location or land survey   A document that shows a property's boundaries and measurements, and specifies the location of the buildings.

Certificate of status   Also called an Estoppel certificate, a document that outlines a condominium corporation's financial and legal state.

Closed mortgage   A mortgage with a locked-in payment schedule that doesn't vary over the life of the closed term. Holders of closed mortgages may have to pay the lender a penalty to repay the loan before the end of the term.

Closing costs Costs associated with purchasing a home, including legal fees and land transfer taxes, that are payable on the closing date. These costs typically range from 2 to 3 per cent of selling price.

Closing date The date when the transfer of ownership of a property becomes final.

CMHC insurance premiums CMHC mortgage loan insurance premium is calculated as a percentage of the mortgage and based on the size of down payment. The higher the percentage of the total house price/value borrowed, the higher the percentage buyers will pay in insurance premiums.

Compound interest Interest calculated on both the principal and accrued interest of a mortgage.

Conditional offer An Offer to Purchase that is subject to conditions, such as passing a house inspection or arranging financing, and usually valid for a specific period of time.

Condominium (also known as strata) A high-rise, low-rise, or townhouse unit that can be owned, with the individual unit owners sharing ownership rights for the common space of the building, including the outdoor grounds and facilities such as a swimming pool and fitness centre. Unit owners control the common areas through an owners' association.

Contractor A person or company responsible for construction or renovation of a property, including managing suppliers and subcontractors.

Conventional mortgage A mortgage up to a maximum of 80 per cent of a property's value. Mortgage insurance is not required for this type of mortgage.

Counter-offer If a prospective buyer's original offer on a property is not accepted by the seller, the vendor may counter-offer, usually by amending the price, closing date, or another inclusion.

Covenant A clause in a legal document that, in the case of a mortgage, gives the parties to the mortgage a right or an obligation. For example, a covenant can impose the obligation on a borrower to make mortgage payments in certain amounts on certain dates. A mortgage document consists of covenants agreed to by the borrower and the lender.

Credit bureau A company that collects information from various sources and provides a summary on a person's credit history, namely their borrowing and paying habits.

Credit history or report   The report a lender uses to determine a prospective borrower's credit worthiness, including information about their ability to manage debt and their outstanding credit obligations.

Curb appeal   The attractiveness of a property from the street or front view, assessing the exterior maintenance and landscaping of a home.

Deed   A legal document, signed by both buyer and seller, transferring ownership.

Deposit   Money placed in trust by the buyer when making an Offer to Purchase, which is then held by the real estate representative or lawyer until the sale is closed, at which time it is paid to the seller.

Depreciation   The decrease in the value of a property over time.

Down payment   The amount of money a buyer puts toward the purchase of a property, with the balance of the purchase price financed by a mortgage loan. Currently in Canada, in most cases, buyers of investment properties must have a minimum 20 per cent down payment. Buyers of primary homes generally must have a minimum five per cent down payment.

Duplex   A building with two single-family homes. In most major Canadian cities, the term describes only homes located one above the other.

Equity   The difference between the value of a property and what the owner owes on the mortgage.

Fixed mortgage rate   An interest rate that is locked in and will not increase over the term of the mortgage.

Foreclosure   The legal process whereby the lender takes possession of a property because the owner is in default of the mortgage, and the lender sells the property to cover the debts.

Freehold   A term describing outright ownership of property, as is usually the case with detached and semi-detached homes, duplexes, and townhouses. Freehold owners are free to do as they wish with their property, though they must respect building codes, municipal bylaws, and provincial and federal laws.

Gross debt service ratio   The percentage of a borrower's gross monthly income that will be used for monthly payments of principal, interest, taxes, and heating costs, as well as half of the maintenance fees in condo ownership.

Gross monthly income   A person's monthly income before taxes and deductions.

High-ratio mortgage   A mortgage higher than 80 per cent of the lending value of the property, which usually requires high-ratio mortgage insurance from Canada Mortgage and Housing Corporation or another approved lender.

Home inspector   A professional who inspects a home to assess the condition of the structure and its major components and operating systems, including roofing, furnace, and foundation. An inspection report will highlight any issues or necessary repairs.

Interest   The cost of borrowing money from a lender, usually paid in regular payments along with portions of the principal loan amount.

Interest rate   The price, as a percentage, that a borrower pays a lender for the use of money.

Land registration   A legal document that records the ownership of property.

Land surveyor   A professional who surveys a property to provide a certificate of location.

Land transfer tax   The tax paid to the provincial and/or municipal governments for transferring a property from the seller to the buyer.

Lender   A bank, trust company, credit union, financial institution, or private lender that lends money for a mortgage.

Lien   A claim against a property for money owing, usually filed by a supplier or subcontractor.

Link home (also known as carriage home)   Two individual homes joined by a garage or basement walls so the houses appear to be a single-family home. They are usually less expensive than fully detached units.

Loan-to-value ratio (LTV)   The ratio of a loan to the lending value of a property, as a percentage.

Lump sum prepayment   An extra payment to reduce the principal balance of a mortgage, made with or without penalty. A closed mortgage typically restricts the amount and frequency of prepayments. An open mortgage typically allows lump sum prepayments at any time without penalty. Prepayments can help borrowers pay off their mortgage sooner, with significant savings.

Maturity date   The last day of the term of a mortgage, when the mortgage must either be paid in full or the agreement renewed.

Mortgage   A mortgage is a security for a loan to buy a property, repaid in regular payments that include the principal (amount borrowed) plus interest.

Mortgage approval   Written notification from a lender to a borrower that approves the advancement of a specified amount of mortgage funds under specified conditions.

Mortgage broker   A professional who searches among a variety of mortgage lenders and products to find terms and rates that suit a borrower.

Mortgage default   Failure to make a mortgage payment.

Mortgage delinquency   Failure to make a mortgage payment on time.

Mortgage discharge   A document a lender presents to a borrower to signify a mortgage has been repaid in full.

Mortgage life insurance   Life insurance coverage of a borrower and his or her family; in the event of the borrower's death, the mortgage is paid off.

Mortgage loan insurance   Insurance coverage on holders of a high-ratio mortgage (more than 80 per cent of the lending value of a property) that will likely be required by their lender.

Mortgage payment   A regular payment to the lender that comprises principal and interest.

Mortgage term   The length of time that a mortgage contract's conditions, including interest rate, is fixed.

Multiple Listing Service (MLS®)   A co-operative service owned and controlled by real estate boards (in Canada, the Canadian Real Estate Association) and used by realtors, which contains descriptions of homes listed for sale.

Net worth   A person's financial worth, calculated by subtracting liabilities from assets.

New home warranty (New Home Warranty Program)   A guarantee that if something covered under the warranty needs to be repaired, it will be.

If the builder doesn't repair it, the repair will be done by the organization that provided the warranty.

Offer to Purchase A written contract setting out the terms under which a buyer agrees to buy a property. If the Offer to Purchase is accepted by the seller, it forms a legally binding contract.

Open house A period of time during which a property for sale is held open for viewing to prospective buyers, usually one or two days on a weekend.

Open mortgage A flexible mortgage that allows the borrower to pay part of the loan before the end of its term.

Operating costs The monthly expenses to operate a home, including property taxes, insurance, utilities, maintenance, and repairs.

Payment schedule The monthly, biweekly, or weekly intervals in which mortgage payments are made.

PITH Principal, interest, taxes, and heating—costs lenders use to calculate gross debt service ratio (GDS).

Principal The amount of money a person borrows from a lender.

Property insurance Insurance that affords owners financial reimbursement in the event a property suffers damage due to fire or other hazards.

Property taxes Taxes charged by the municipality where the home is located, based on the value of the home.

Real estate Real property consisting of houses or commercial buildings and land.

Realtor or real estate agent A licensed professional who acts as an intermediary between the seller and the buyer of a property.

Refinance To pay off a mortgage and arrange for financing, sometimes with a different lender.

Renewal The act of renegotiating a loan for a new term, when the previous term expires.

Rental rate The dollar amount a tenant agrees to pay to live in a property.

Reserve fund In the context of a condo ownership, a fund set aside by the condominium corporation for emergency or major repairs.

Rowhouse (also known as townhouse) One unit of several similar single-family homes, side-by-side, joined by common walls.

Second mortgage A second mortgage on a property that already has a first mortgage.

Seller's market Market conditions when supply of property is insufficient to meet demand. Prices may increase, homes sell quickly, and sellers have more leverage.

Single-family detached home Free-standing home for one family, not attached to another property on either side.

Single-family semi-detached home Home for one family, attached to another building on one side.

Stacked townhouse Two two-storey homes are stacked one on top of the other, usually attached in groups of four or more.

Title A freehold title gives the holder exclusive ownership of a property for an indefinite period. A leasehold title gives the holder the right to use a property for a defined period.

Title insurance Insurance against loss or damage caused by a matter affecting the title to immoveable property, such as a lien, encumbrance, or servitude.

Total debt service (TDS) ratio The percentage of a person's gross monthly income required to cover the monthly housing payments and other debts, such as car payments.

Townhouse (also known as rowhouse) One unit of several similar single-family homes, side-by-side, joined by common walls.

Vacancy rate Percentage of rentable units remaining unoccupied.

Variable mortgage rate An interest rate that fluctuates over the term of the mortgage, based on market conditions. The mortgage payment remains unchanged.

Vendor A seller of a property.

Vendor take-back mortgage The vendor of a property, not a financial institution, finances the mortgage. The property is transferred to the buyer, who makes mortgage payments directly to the seller.

Zoning Municipal or regional laws that restrict land to a specific use.

Appendix C: Sample Offer Clauses and Conditions

The following is a selection of sample clauses and conditions that can be inserted into offers. Seek independent legal advice before inserting any clause to make sure you fully understand the clause and its implications.

Right to Assign Agreement

The Buyer shall have the right at any time prior to closing, to assign the within Offer to any person, persons or corporation, either existing or to be incorporated, and upon delivery to the Seller of notice of such assignment, together with the assignee's covenant in favour of the Seller to be bound hereby as Buyer, the Buyer hereinbefore named shall stand released from all further liability hereunder.

Condition – Severance – Seller Undertakes Expense and Completion

This Offer is conditional upon the Buyer obtaining, at the Seller's expense, a consent to sever the property as follows: [provide description of proposed severance]. Unless the Buyer gives notice in writing delivered to the Seller not later than _____ p.m. on the _____ day of _____, 20_____, that this condition is fulfilled, this Offer shall become null and void and the deposit shall be returned to the Buyer in full without deduction. This condition is included for the benefit of the Buyer and may be waived at the Buyer's sole option by notice in writing to the Seller within the time period stated herein.

The Seller understands and acknowledges that the Seller shall be responsible for satisfying any conditions imposed, and if such conditions give the Seller options in the manner of compliance, the Buyer shall determine which option will be selected. The Seller shall obtain a reference plan prepared by an Ontario Land Surveyor suitable for registration purposes in the Land Registry Office in which the said property is located.

Condition – All Environmental Laws Complied With

This Offer is conditional upon the Buyer determining, at the Buyer's own expense, that: all environmental laws and regulations have been complied with, no hazardous conditions or substances exist on the land, no limitations or restrictions affecting the continued use of the property exist, other than those specifically provided for herein, no pending litigation respecting Environmental matters, no outstanding Ministry of Environment Orders, investigation, charges or prosecutions respecting Environmental matters exist, there has been no prior use as a waste disposal site, and all applicable licences are in force. The Seller agrees to provide to the Buyer upon request, all documents, records, and reports relating to environmental matters in possession of the Seller. The Seller further authorizes [insert appropriate Ministry], to release to the Buyer, the Buyer's Agent or Solicitor, any and all information that may be on record in the Ministry office with respect to the said property.

Unless the Buyer gives notice in writing delivered to the Seller not later than _____ p.m. on the _____ day of _____, 20____, that the preceding condition has been fulfilled, this Offer shall become null and void and the deposit shall be returned to the Buyer in full without deduction. This condition is included for the benefit of the Buyer and may be waived at the Buyer's sole option by notice in writing to the Seller within the time period stated herein.

Environmental Issues – Release of Documents from Appropriate Ministries

The Seller authorizes the [insert appropriate Ministry] to release to the Buyer, or the Buyer's Representative or Solicitor, any and all information that may be on record in the Ministry's office with respect to the said property.

Environmental Warranty – All Laws Complied With

The Seller represents and warrants to the best of the Seller's knowledge and belief that during the period of his ownership of the property, that: all environmental laws and regulations have been complied with, no hazardous conditions or substances exist on the land, no limitations or restrictions affecting the continued use of the property exist, other than those specifically provided for herein, no pending litigation respecting Environmental matters; no outstanding Ministry of Environment Orders, investigations, charges or prosecutions regarding Environmental matters exist, there has been no prior use as a waste disposal site, and all applicable licences are in force. The Seller agrees to provide to the Buyer upon request, all documents, records, and reports relating to environmental matters that are in the possession of the Seller. The Seller further authorizes [insert appropriate Ministry], to release to the Buyer, the Buyer's Agent or Solicitor, any and all information that may be on record in the Ministry office with respect to the said property.

The Parties agree that this representation and warranty shall form an integral part of this Agreement and survive the completion of this transaction, but apply only to circumstances existing at completion of this transaction.

No Growth or Manufacture of Illegal Substances – Warranty

The Seller represents and warrants that during the time the Seller has owned the property, the use of the property and the buildings and structures thereon has not been for the growth or manufacture of any illegal substances, and that to the best of the Seller's knowledge and belief, the use of the property and the buildings and structures thereon has never been for the growth or manufacture of illegal substances. This warranty shall survive and not merge on the completion of this transaction.

Delivery of Documents

Any notice relating hereto or provided for herein shall be in writing. This Offer, any counter offer, notice of acceptance thereof, or any notice shall be deemed given and received, when hand delivered to the address for service provided herein or, where a facsimile number is provided herein, when transmitted electronically to that facsimile number or via e-mail.

H.S.T. Buyer is Registrant (Commercial Component)

The Buyer shall deliver to the Seller on closing:

1. a statutory declaration that the Buyer is a registrant within the meaning of Part IX of the Excise Tax Act of Canada (the "Act") and that the Buyer's registration is in full force and effect;

2. reasonable evidence of the Buyer's registration under the Act; and

3. an undertaking by the Buyer to remit any tax eligible under the Act in respect of this transaction and to indemnify the Seller against all loss, costs and damages resulting from the Buyer's failure to do so.

Ontario Heritage Act Designation

The parties hereto acknowledge that the subject property is/may be designated as a Heritage Property and is subject to the provisions of The Ontario Heritage Act, 1974. The Buyer acknowledges that the Seller has made this disclosure. The Buyer accepts the property with this designation and agrees to continue with this transaction.

Condition – Inspection of Property by a Home Inspector – General Inspection

This Offer is conditional upon the inspection of the subject property by a home inspector at the Buyer's own expense, and the obtaining of a report satisfactory to the Buyer in the Buyer's sole and absolute discretion. Unless the Buyer gives notice in writing delivered to the Seller not later than 5 business days following acceptance of this Agreement, that this condition is fulfilled, this Offer shall be null and void and the deposit shall be returned to the Buyer in full without deduction. The Seller agrees to co-operate in providing access to the property for the purpose of this inspection. This condition is included for the benefit of the Buyer and may be waived at the Buyer's sole and absolute option by notice in writing to the Seller within the time period stated herein.

Condition – Arranging Insurance

This offer is conditional on the Buyer arranging insurance for the property satisfactory to the Buyer in the Buyer's sole and absolute discretion. Unless the Buyer gives notice in writing delivered to the Seller not later than _____ p.m. on the _____ day of _____, 20_____, that this condition is fulfilled, this offer shall be null and void and the deposit shall be returned to the Buyer in full without deduction. The Seller agrees to co-operate in providing access to the property, if necessary, for any inspection of the property required for the fulfillment of this condition. This condition is included for the benefit of the Buyer and may be waived at the Buyer's sole option by notice in writing to the Seller within the time period stated herein.

Condition – Lawyer's Approval – Buyer

This Offer is conditional upon the approval of the terms hereof by the Buyer's Solicitor. Unless the Buyer gives notice in writing delivered to the Seller not later than _____ p.m. on the _____ day of _____, 20_____, that this condition is fulfilled, this Offer shall be null and void and the deposit shall be returned to the Buyer in full without deduction. This condition is included for the benefit of Buyer and may be waived at the Buyer's sole option by notice in writing to the Seller within the time period stated herein.

Condition – Lawyer's Approval – Seller

This Offer is conditional upon the approval of the terms hereof by the Seller's Solicitor. Unless the Seller gives notice in writing delivered to the Buyer or to the Buyer's address as hereinafter indicated not later than _____ p.m. on the _____ day of _____, 20_____, that this condition is fulfilled, this Offer shall be null and void and the deposit shall be returned to the Buyer in full without deduction. This condition is included for the benefit of Seller and may be waived at the Seller's sole option by notice in writing to the Buyer within the time period stated herein.

Condition – Inspection of Leases and Real Property— (Condition Subsequent)

This Agreement is conditional upon the Buyer inspecting and approving the real property, the Leases (or Offers to Lease if no Leases are available), and improvements. Unless the Buyer notifies the Seller or the Seller's agents in writing by not later than _____ p.m. on the _____ day of _____, 20_____, that the Buyer is not satisfied with any of the above inspections, the

Buyer shall be deemed to have waived this condition and this Agreement shall remain valid and binding.

The Seller agrees to:

a) Supply the Buyer not later than _____ p.m. on the _____ day of _____, 20_____, with all Leases and/or Offers to Lease which are in force at the time of acceptance of this Offer and a set of "as built" building plans for the development of the site (if such are in its possession);

b) Allow the Buyer, its agents and employees, to inspect the land and improvements at mutually convenient time or times; and

c) Authorize all governmental and other authorities having jurisdiction over the real property to release to the Buyer all information such authorities have on file respecting the property.

Should the Buyer hire agents, the cost and responsibility of such work shall be for the account of the Buyer. The Buyer covenants and agrees to restore the property forthwith after inspection to its pre-existing physical condition prior to the time of the first such inspection.

If the Buyer is not satisfied with the results of the Buyer's inspection, the Buyer shall so notify the Seller, who may elect to remedy such results. If the Seller does not remedy such results to the satisfaction of the Buyer, the Buyer may terminate this Agreement by notice in writing delivered to the Seller not later than _____ p.m. on the _____ day of _____, 20_____, and the deposit shall be returned to the Buyer in full without deduction.

The Buyer agrees to treat the results of such inspections in a strictly confidential manner and not to disclose the results to a third party except where required by law. There shall be no compulsory requirement to disclose the result to the Seller.

Seller Take-Back Mortgage – Simple Interest Only

The Seller agrees to take back a _____ Charge/Mortgage [for the balance of the Purchase price] OR [in the amount of _____ ($_____)] bearing interest at the rate of _____% per annum, repayable interest only _____

[state payment interval, e.g., monthly, quarterly, etc.] and maturing on the
_____ day of _____, 20_____.

The Chargee hereby acknowledges that the chargor has prepaid three months interest in advance in the amount of $_____, based on $_____.00 being advanced on the registration date, as agreed upon between the parties of this charge. Interest will be payable, monthly, based on the principal amount advanced.

In the event the chargor should sell, assign or transfer the charged premises the principal balance outstanding at the time of such sale, assignment or transfer together with accrued interest shall be forthwith become due and payable. The mortgagor has the privilege of prepaying the whole or any part of the principal sum secured at any time or times without notice or bonus after three months.

The Chargor shall provide the Chargee with a series of 9 post-dated cheques at the commencement of this Charge. The mortgagor has the privilege of prepaying the whole or any part of the principal sum secured after three months at any time or times without notice or bonus.

In the event that any cheque presented for payment is not honoured for any reason whatsoever, the Chargor covenants and agrees to pay to the Chargee an administrative charge of $250.00.

In the event any cheque is late there shall be a fee of $100.00 for each late payment.

Increase of Rent with Notices Prior to Completion of Sale

The Seller shall, at the earliest legally permitted time to completion, give notices of rent increases, at the statutory rate or as otherwise agreed between the Buyer and the Seller, and provide the Buyer with proof of proper service thereof.

No Rent Increases Pending Completion of Sale

Pending completion, the Seller shall not give any notices of rent increases.

Notices to Tenants of New Owner

Upon completion, the Seller shall provide the Buyer with a notice to all tenants advising them of the new owner and requiring all future rents to be paid as the Buyer directs. The Seller will pay to the Buyer any rent paid to the Seller in error or in violation of the direction for a period of _____ months following completion, after which period the Seller may refuse to accept rent from tenants or return it to them.

Rent – No Warranty Re Legality of Rents

The Seller represents and warrants, to the best of the Seller's knowledge and belief, that the current actual rents are:

Unit	Current Rent	Last Increase (Date/Amount)
_____	_____	_____
_____	_____	_____

The Parties agree that this representation and warranty shall survive and not merge on completion of this transaction, but apply only to those circumstances existing at completion of this transaction. The Parties also agree that the warranty given is as to actual rents only, and does not extend to the legality of the rents.

Rent – General Warranty by Seller

The Seller represents and warrants, to the best of the Seller's knowledge and belief that, during the period of the Seller's ownership, the property has been rented in accordance with Landlord and Tenant legislation and that any rent increase has been effected in accordance with relevant rent review legislation. The Parties agree that this representation and warranty shall survive and not merge on completion of this transaction, but apply only to those circumstances existing at completion of this transaction.

Rent – Seller Warranty Regarding Disputes

The Seller represents and warrants, to the best of the Seller's knowledge and belief, that there are no disputes between the Seller as landlord and any tenant as to the state of repair of the leased premises, the payment of rents, contravention of applicable rent review legislation for residential tenancies, or other material items concerning the tenants' lease agreements other than as specifically set out in this Agreement of Purchase and Sale. The Parties agree that these representations and warranties shall survive and not merge on completion of this transaction, but apply only to those circumstances existing at completion of this transaction.

Seller to Provide Existing Survey with Declaration

The Seller agrees to provide, at the Seller's own expense, not later than
_____p.m. on the _____ day of _____, 20_____, an existing survey of
said property showing the current location of all structures, buildings,
fences, improvements, easements, rights-of-way, and encroachments
affecting said property. The Seller will further deliver, on completion, a
declaration confirming that there have been no additions to the structures, buildings, fences, and improvements on the property since the
date of this survey.

Assessment/Changes in Property Tax Amounts Due to Re-assessment

The Buyer and Seller hereby acknowledge that the [insert appropriate
province] has implemented current value assessment and properties may
be re-assessed on an annual basis. The Buyer and Seller agree that no claim
will be made against the Buyer or Seller, or any Broker or Salesperson, for
any changes in property tax as a result of a re-assessment of the property.

Condition – Rezoning/Minor Variance

This Offer is conditional upon the [Buyer/Seller] obtaining at the [Buyer's/
Seller's] expense, a [rezoning/minor variance], to allow for [specify exact
variance/use] for said property. Both Buyer and Seller agree to proceed in
a diligent manner to acquire the [rezoning/minor variance]. Unless the
[Buyer/Seller] gives notice in writing delivered to the [Seller/Buyer] not
later than _____ p.m. on the _____ day of _____, 20_____, that this
condition is fulfilled, this Offer shall become null and void and the deposit
shall be returned to the Buyer in full without deduction.

Inclusions

It is agreed and understood that all existing flooring and floor cov-
erings, drapery tracks, ceiling fans and fixtures, built-in appliances,
heating-ventilating and air conditioning equipment, and all other items
secured by means of nails, screws, plumbing, wiring, ducting and related
accessories, thereto now on the real property are to be included in the
purchase price except items which are leased or rented and those specifically listed herein.

Property Survey

The Seller agrees to provide the Buyer with a copy of the existing survey for the subject property, as well as a properly executed OREA Seller Property Information Statement within 24 hours of acceptance of this offer, which shall form part of this agreement of purchase and sale.

Property Visits

The Buyer shall have the right to three visits prior to completion. The said visits are to be a mutually agreed upon, following the verbal request for such visits.

Chattels and Fixtures

The Seller represents and warrants that the chattels and fixtures as included in this Agreement of Purchase and Sale will be in good working order and free from all liens and encumbrances on completion. The Parties agree that this representation and warranty shall survive and not merge on completion of this transaction, but apply only to the state of the property at completion of this transaction.

Appendix D: Property Analyzer

123 Street Avenue Road

Location:
Listing:

Fixtures/Equipment:
Features:
Comments:

						Instructions
Purchase Price					$184,000	Enter your purchase price.
Financing Information					**Amount**	
1st Mortgage			80%		$147,200	Enter the % of your requested 1st mortgage.
2nd Mortgage			0%		$0	Enter the % of your requested 2nd mortgage.
Investment					**Amount**	
Down Payment					$36,800	Automatically calculated (Purchase Price - Total Mortgages).
Land Transfer Tax					$1,565	Automatically calculated.
Immediate Repairs and Renovations					$5,000	Enter the total amount of your estimated repairs and renovations.
Inspection					$371	Enter the cost of having the property inspected.
Appraisal					$239	Enter the cost of having the property appraised.
Title Insurance					$266	Enter the cost of having a survey completed, if applicable.
Financing Costs					$0	Enter the total amount of lender and mortgage broker fees.
Legal Costs (Including Disbursements)					$1,840	Enter the total amount of legal fees, including disbursements and title insurance.
Staying Power Fund (2mo rent)					$4,000	Automatically calculated (one month's rent). Can be overwritten.
Other					$0	Enter any additional costs or fees associated with this property.
Total Investment					$50,081	Automatically calculated.

Income				**Monthly**	**Annually**	
Gross Rents				$2,000.00	$24,000	Enter the total monthly rents that you expect from the property.
Laundry				$0.00	$0	Enter the total monthly laundry income you expect from the property.
Other Rents				$0.00	$360	Enter the total monthly amount you expect from other rents such as storage.
Total Income				$2,000.00	$24,360	Automatically calculated.

Operating Expenses			%	**Monthly**	**Annually**	
Heating				$0.00	$0	Enter the expected monthly costs for heating, if applicable.
Electricity				$0.00	$0	Enter the expected monthly costs for electricity, if applicable.
Water / Sewer				$0.00	$0	Enter the expected monthly costs for water or sewer, if applicable.
Property Taxes				$170.00	$2,040	Enter the annual property taxes.
Condo Fees (if applicable)				$0.00	$0	Enter the monthly condo fees, if applicable.
Insurance				$100.00	$1,200	Enter the annual premium for property insurance.
Property Management			5.0%	$100.00	$1,200	Enter the % for property management, if applicable.
Rental Pool Management			0.0%	$0.00	$0	Enter the % for rental pool management, if applicable.
Repairs and Maintenance			5.0%	$100.00	$1,200	Enter the % for repairs and maintenance.
Resident Manager				$0.00	$0	Enter the monthly cost for a resident manager, if applicable.
Snow Removal				$0.00	$0	Enter the annual cost for snow removal, if applicable.
Lawn Maintenance				$0.00	$0	Enter the annual cost for lawn maintenance, if applicable.
Pest Control				$0.00	$0	Enter the annual cost for pest control, if applicable.
Other (e.g rented equipment: hot water heater)				$0.00	$0	Enter the monthly cost for any other expenses.
Total Operating Expenses				$470.00	$5,640	Automatically calculated.

Operating Income			%	**Monthly**	**Annually**	
Operating Income				$1,530.00	$18,720	Automatically calculated (NOI / Total Mortgage Payments)
Less: Vacancy Allowance			5.0%	$100.00	$1,200	Enter the % for vacancy allowance.
Net Operating Income (NOI)				$1,430.00	$17,520	Automatically calculated.

Financing Costs	**Type**	**Amort**	**Rate**	**Monthly**	**Annually**	
1st Mortgage Payment	P + I	35	4.50%	$692.84	$8,314	Enter the expected interest rate on the 1st mortgage.
2nd Mortgage Payment	Int Only	25	3.00%	$0.00	$0	Enter the expected interest rate on the 2nd mortgage.
Total Financing Payments				$692.84	$8,314	Automatically calculated.

Cash Flow				**Monthly**	**Annually**	
Cash Flow Before Taxes				$737.16	$9,206	Automatically calculated (NOI - Total Financing Payments).
CAP Rate (ROA)					9.52%	Automatically calculated (NOI / Purchase Price).
Debt Coverage Ratio (DSR) - Your View					2.11	Automatically calculated (NOI / Total Financing Payments).
Debt Coverage Ratio (DSR) - Lender's View					2.06	DCR the way the lender calculates it.

Return on Investment			**Rate**	**Amount**	**Return**	
Cash Return				$9,205.86	18.38%	Automatically calculated (Cash Flow Before Taxes / Investment).
Mortgage Paydown				$1,787.63	3.57%	Automatically calculated (Mortgage Paydown / Investment).
Appreciation			5.0%	$9,200.00	18.37%	Enter your expected appreciation % (Appreciation Amount / Investment).
Total Return on Investment (ROI)					40.32%	Automatically calculated.

Appendix E: Contact Information

AUTHOR

Tahani Aburaneh
Email: tahani@tahani.ca
Websites:
   www.realestaterichesbook.com
   www.keyconnexions.ca
Facebook: Tahani Aburaneh
Twitter: @TahaniAburaneh
LinkedIn: Tahani Aburaneh

WRITER

Wayne Karl
wkarl@rogers.com

CONTRIBUTORS

Thomas Beyer – www.prestprop.com
Kevin Boughen – www.investormortgages.ca
Mike Cunning – www.upcountrygroup.com
George E. Dube – www.dubecuttini.com
Wade Graham – www.hgrei.com

Adam Hoffman – www.hoffaco.com
Philip G. Jarvie – www.hubinternational.com
Peter Kinch – www.peterkinch.com
Mark Loeffler – www.theversatileinvestor.com
Todd Millar and Danielle Millar – www.glennsimoninc.com
Dave Peniuk – www.revnyou.com
Brian Pulis – www.pulisinvestments.com
Joe Ragona – www.engagedinvestor.ca
Shayle Rothman – www.realestatelawyers.ca
Ben Sanderson – www.dreamhometoday.ca
Pierre-Paul Turgeon – www.matterhorninvesting.com
Neil Uttamsingh – www.firstrentalproperty.com
Cindy Wennerstrom – www.oroproperties.ca
Russell Westcott – www.reincanada.com

Index